Quantity Planning and Price Planning in the Soviet Union

Quantity Planning and Price Planning in the Soviet Union

by Hans Hirsch

*Translated from the German
by Karl Scholz
Emeritus Professor of Economics
University of Pennsylvania*

*Edited by William N. Loucks
Professor of Economics
University of Pennsylvania*

Philadelphia
University of Pennsylvania Press

© 1961, by The Trustees of the University of Pennsylvania

Published in Great Britain, India, and Pakistan
by the Oxford University Press
London, Bombay, and Karachi

Library of Congress Catalogue Card Number 61-5541

Printed in the United States of America

Contents

Introduction

Introduction

THE QUESTION of economic accounting under socialism has
attracted much interest for a long time. This is primarily
due to its key position in the controversy over the economic
order. However, if understood correctly, it is just as important to pure economic theory. Here lies the best opportunity first to examine price theory statements and to
perceive how far price theory has either general validity
or is merely applicable to particular historical phenomena,
and secondly, to separate out the items that are not determined by the logic of the theoretical system but by the
incidental peculiarities of the empirical economy to which
the theory is related.

This significance of the question has been recognized for
a long time. In the first contributions to the subject,
especially in the well-known article by Enrico Barone on
"Production Administration in the Collectivised State," it
was not a matter of choosing a type of economic order but
of determining the area of validity of a theory. However,
for a long time it was not possible to find support in practical experiences, i.e., in executed economic planning
attempts; rather it was first necessary to develop a purely

theoretical planned economic system. But relating the theory to practical experiences raises doubts on the one hand that may mislead one to interpret the incidental features of a historical phenomenon as general characteristics of an economic system. On the other hand, only by evaluating practical experiences is it possible to avoid purely exotic theoretical structures. The posed question cannot be answered by referring to an imaginable system, but must be related to an attainable socialistic or planned economic system. Such a practical attempt reveals the difficulties but also the specific possibilities of such a system. Hence the planned economic experiment that was undertaken in the Soviet Union is highly interesting, solely from the standpoint of economic theory and aside from every political and ideologic consideration. Conceivably much valuable insight can be obtained from Soviet experiences, especially negative experiences, and particularly from the difficulties that have been encountered.

A first and significant result pertinent to economic theory dealing with economic planning is the distinction between the internal consistency of the economic value system and the origin of final goal-setting. This refers to the separation of the question of economic accounting from that of "consumer sovereignty." Mixing these two concepts has caused much confusion in the area of the topics treated here. It is typical of hasty generalization of conclusions reached on the basis of the theory of a particular market economy. The same may be said of the theory of the public economy within the framework of the market economy. Price theory in its narrow interpretation was hitherto not applicable to it, and hence has long been in need of this extension.

A second problem, it seems to me, has been considered

inadequately. It deals with the relationship between planning in kind (material planning) and financial economic guidance, aided by a price system. Authors who have dealt with the conceptual development of the possibilities of price calculation under socialism have logically developed a certain antipathy toward the thought of material planning. In order to meet the charge of neglecting the optimum concept that is necessarily connected with material planning as such, they endeavored to show that a planned economic system need not be planned in kind, and developed a purely financial planned economic guidance system. The doubt as to this extreme point of view arises from the fact that the idea of economic planning originally was attractive partly because of the hope that, with its aid, general economic coordinating defects (crises and unemployment) arising out of the operation of the money system would be overcome, in which connection the thought of material coordination of individual measures played a part from the outset. The question is, therefore, whether the absolute antithesis between material planning and financial guidance is really justified, or whether it is not possible to combine both methods of guidance into one system.

The clarification of this question is impossible if based solely on theoretical postulates. The purely deductive concept of a material guidance system is too hazy and burdened with too many reservations of a conjectural nature. Hence, the guidance system of the Soviet Union affords opportunity to examine an extensively developed, even though not complete, material guidance system. We can here obtain for the time being a specific view of the possibilities and problems of such a guidance system. At the same time, the observer who occupies himself with this system will see that material planning is so important in a positive sense that its abandonment in favor of purely financial guidance methods is scarcely imaginable.

On the other hand, Soviet experiences confirm the significance of the price system of financial guidance methods even for the planned economy, and hence justify its introduction into the theory. Its exposition has been the primary objective of this study. There is still considerable lack of clarity as to this point. It can be traced chiefly to Soviet attitudes toward this question, for, as will be shown, they are not altogether clear there as to what is being done. The fundamental pronouncements, especially, are very firmly tied to the prescribed dogma system and, in each case, one must distinguish carefully between effective guidance concepts and mere dogmatic "superstructure."

How is the position of prices within the framework of a material guidance system to be interpreted? Thus far, Western thought has regarded material and financial guidance methods as incompatible and in opposition to each other. Such a conclusion would be very unfortunate for practical planning, for the reasons given. Hence it seems important to me to note that a trend toward a purposively coordinated price system need not confine itself to financial guidance methods exclusively, i.e., that the immediate production guiding agencies are guided solely by financial criteria. Thus one may hope to combine the advantages of material balance methods and the clarification of the planning process with the aid of financial criteria into a single guidance system. Theoretically, at least, there can be no objections to doing so.

Moreover, the presentation of the guidance system per se should be of interest, aside from the inferences of economic theory. Soviet authors generally discuss only the why, not the how, of economic planning. The available material on the Soviet economy relative to this second and really economic question is intriguing. If, as I hope, the theoretical inquiry also proves fruitful as the central thought in this presentation, its introduction is justified.*

Author's Supplementary Note

DURING PUBLICATION certain changes have become known. A certain relaxation of the official attitude toward price planning is indicated, combined with a more open discussion, in general, of planning principles. In this connection see the reports of Davies and Schlesinger in *Soviet Studies,* Vol. 8, pp. 426-436, and Vol. 9, pp. 92-98 respectively (particularly interesting is the appearance of the marginal cost problem discussed by Davies, pp. 434 f. and Schlesinger, p. 95).

More significant is the reorganization of the entire planning and guidance apparatus, decreed in May of 1957 and rapidly put into effect. In place of industry branches according to ministries, spatial administration now appears as the highest organizational principle, consisting of 105 administrative economic districts, each under an Economic Council. Industrial ministries have been discontinued almost entirely. Corresponding to the office of chief administration, branch administrations are established, wherever necessary, in the area of an individual Economic Council. These specialize to a degree roughly equal to that of the former ministries. The State Economic Commission

* Acknowledgments and methods of transcribing Russian titles and concepts into German appear in the Preface to the English translation. These have been omitted here.

has again been discontinued or combined with *Gosplan* (again called "State Planning Committee") into one organization. The system continues of unified planning for the entire area of the Soviet Union with the aid of material balances and the supply plans based on them. However, the weight of participating agencies is shifted. In the first place, regional balances of smaller areas, which formerly had only limited effectiveness, now attain particular importance. Aside from the decentralizing tendency of the entire reform, the increasing influence of lower agencies is indicated by the fact that the planning process is again to begin from below, with the enterprises. Also, there is to be a steady reduction in the number of items in the all-Union balances (centralized funds) in contrast with the former situation. Furthermore, in the economic plan of the Union, many final tasks and items are to be fixed only in aggregate form for the Union Republics, and then broken down by them. Particularly, this permits the *Gosplan* of the Russian Soviet Federative Socialist Republic (RSFSR), which embraces 70 of the 105 economic regions, to exercise considerable influence. (The Ukrainian Union Republic embraces 11 economic regions, and most of the other Union republics represent single economic regions.) On the other hand, the connection between Economic Councils and the plan, and particularly the deliveries required of them to other regions, are emphasized. Major decisions continue to be made by the all-Union *Gosplan* as, for example, confirmation of projects beyond established limits, but the limit for all such smaller projects is raised to 50 million rubles. Planned tasks and allocation plans are subject to a more detailed calculation in the all-Union *Gosplan,* even where they are confirmed in the plan merely as aggregates for the Union republics. Of particular significance for the

limitation of influence will be the composition of the allocation apparatus. The marketing and supply divisions (i.e.,
chief administrations) (*glavsbyt* and *glavsneb*) of the ministries have not been dissolved, but have, "for the time being,"
been combined partly with the all-Union *Gosplan,* and
partly with that of the RSFSR, etc. On the other hand,
their foreign offices have likewise been transferred "for the
time being" to the economic councils which, at all events,
are also to reorganize the allocation apparatus. Final decisions have not yet been reached here. Lastly, the division
of influence between *Gosplan* and Economic Councils will
be just as difficult to fathom as was that previously pertaining to *Gosplan* and ministries. (For all this, see Miller
in *Soviet Studies,* Vol. 9, pp. 63-85 as well as, for details,
see *Planned Economy,* 1957, No. 6, pp. 19 f.; No. 7, pp. 6-9,
pp. 88 f.; No. 8, pp. 38 ff., 87, 89.)

Preface to
English Translation

THIS TRANSLATION of the study *Mengenplanung und Preis-planung in der Sovjetunion* (*Quantity Planning and Price Planning in the Soviet Union*) by Hans Hirsch seeks to reproduce the provocative thesis of the author in concise English. This has been no simple undertaking in view of the many opaque statements and long, involved sentences in the German original. It has at times been necessary to translate lengthy and cumbersome sentences somewhat freely, and to exercise a degree of editorial judgment. The author has played no part in this English rendition. The translator is solely responsible for any possible inaccuracies in interpretation, but every effort has been made to present the author's thesis concisely.

Several bilingual and multilingual colleagues have rendered valuable assistance in interpreting particularly difficult passages appearing in the original. Special acknowledgment of indebtedness for this aid is due to Professor Elsa Ehrenstein of the Faculty of the Philadelphia College of Pharmacy and Science and to Professors Otto Pollak and

Alfred Senn of the Faculty of the University of Pennsylvania. The English translation has been carefully edited by Professor William N. Loucks of the Economics Department of the University of Pennsylvania. In a number of instances he has broken down lengthy, verbose, literally translated statements into short sentences, aimed at clarifying the thoughts expressed in the original. His invaluable services in this connection are herewith acknowledged.

Many of the words and expressions used repeatedly by the author may be variously rendered in English, and different persons have differently translated German terms and expressions relating to the Soviet economy. For example, the expression *"Naturale Lenkungsmethode"* may be variously translated "physical method of directing or guiding" or "method of guiding or directing in kind." Throughout the translation the expression "material guidance method" has been used, in contrast with "financial guidance method" (*finanzieller Lenkungsmethode*). To avoid monotonous repetition of terms often occurring in the original, such words as *"Bindung," "Leistung," "Rechnung," "Pauschalisierung,"* and their derivatives have been translated by various English cognates.

With the author's consent the elaborate footnotes and references in the original have been condensed somewhat, by omitting many references either in support of or in opposition to views expressed in the body of the text. All in all, several hundred such footnote references have been deleted, and usually only the first of long lists of bibliographic references has been given in the translated footnotes and references that appear at the end of the text. Omissions have been indicated by "et al." The footnote titles have all been translated into English, and the foreign language original is indicated by the appropriate letter, such as (R), Russian; (G), German, etc. This general procedure has reduced considerably the space given to footnotes, but wherever a direct quotation occurs in the body of the text the specific source (translated) is shown in the footnote.

Furthermore, certain illustrative materials in Chapter 4, taken largely from secondary sources and somewhat out of date, have been omitted. Where such omission occurs, it has been indicated in a footnote.

Several reviewers of this pioneering work in the theory and practice of quantity and price planning have noted the vagueness of many statements occurring in the original. One reviewer in concluding his critical evaluation observes, ". . . we seem to be wafted into the upper atmosphere of theoretical abstraction without being compensated for the rarefied air by a corresponding absence of haze. This is arduous and disappointing. Nonetheless, we should be grateful for these flights; for there are few prepared to steer us quite so high, and there is evidently much concealed in Mr. Hirsch's haze, which but for such experimental probes, would never be suspected, let alone explored." *

It is hoped that this English translation will serve to stimulate continued inquiry into the validity of the thesis expounded by the author by at least removing a possible linguistic barrier to further research in this field.

Those who benefit from the English translation of this work will owe a debt of gratitude to the University of Pennsylvania Press for undertaking the publication of this volume. The Committee on the Advancement of Research, University of Pennsylvania, has assisted with a grant of funds to pay for typing the manuscript.

Karl Scholz

* F. Seton, "Planning Sub Specie Aeternitatis," *Soviet Studies,* October, 1959, pp. 129-133.

Quantity Planning and Price Planning
in the Soviet Union

⟶⟦ 1 ⟧⟵

Quantity Planning: Balances and Norms

Statement of the Problem

IN THE LITERATURE on Soviet economic planning, the main emphasis is placed on the organization of planning. This part of the subject, which is easily understood by the economically unschooled, has been dealt with almost exclusively by Russian authors. Consequently considerable information is available on this subject. On the other hand, we are interested only in the "What" of economic planning: What determines how much of each good will be produced; how is the choice made between short-term and long-term alternatively producible quantities of goods? In this connection the question of organization may be omitted, insofar as it does not refer substantively to the making of decisions. To be sure, general knowledge of the cooperating agencies and of the manner in which they can influence decisions is significant.

The Russian guidance system utilizes a "method of balances." This may preliminarily be described as follows: It begins with (1) estimates of the desired quantities of goods, and (2) a survey of the production capacities of the available productive resources (including labor) for producing all kinds of goods. With the aid of index numbers, the need for and the producible quantity of each intermediate product (such as raw materials, machinery, semifinished goods, etc.) are computed, step by step, from the highest (final) to the lowest (initial) stage of production. This is prepared in the form of a balance, which becomes a production program only after the requisite checks and balances have been made to assure that production possibilities coincide with production targets.

Obtaining Production Data

Reports from concerns give data on the availability of productive capacities (machinery, plant area, number of employees, gross product, labor productivity, material consumption, etc.). Reports from geographic districts supply data as to the number of workers and employees, natural resources, forests, industrial enterprises and their capacity, agriculture and cultivable area, livestock, machines and trucks, transportation facilities, large-scale building projects, etc.[1] These are aggregated into reports for individual republics and union ministries. The data are corrected periodically to correspond with plan fulfillment for the preceding year (estimated on the basis of the first three quarters). For the allocation of the labor force special balances are planned indicating possible surpluses or deficits in the several economic and industrial branches, and in various categories such as direct labor, supplemental labor, technically trained personnel, and office personnel. These include such supply possibilities as graduates of elementary and industrial-technical schools and employable population, emphasizing possibilities of releases from agriculture.[2]

Economic Goal-Setting

The "directives" of the Central Committee of the Communist Party and the Council of Ministries play the leading role in determining the production goals. Political considerations dictate broad economic goals and ways of attaining them. From these the most important goals are derived and a scale of priorities for the leading branches of industry and directions for their attainment are given. These comprise the fundamental measures for plan fulfillment, as, for example, basic principles of labor organization, price, policy, and distribution.[3]

In accordance with general political objectives of the country, and the resultant economic tasks, the Party and the government decide the most important sections of the plan, for example, the approximate increase in industrial production, the requisite relationship between consumption and accumulation, the necessary relationship between the size of the industrial branches producing the means of production and those producing consumption goods, the development of industrial location, and the specific tasks (building of irrigation systems, power plants, etc.) which it is imperative to carry out. The elaboration of technological development in the impending period is particularly important, since the production program of machine construction and the development potentialities of all other economic branches depend on it.[4]

The actual question is: If and how various possible production and development goals are weighed against each other in drawing up the directives. In this connection, Soviet planning uses the method of "focal point" or "chief link in the chain," i.e., emphasizes chiefly expenditure of economic resources on a top priority goal, which is diametrically opposed to our conception of approximating an optimum by marginal adjustment in all areas of resource utilization. "Leading industrial branches" in this priority sense in the first Five-Year Plan) were chiefly the smelting industry and machine construction, followed by transportation in the second Five-Year Plan, the chemical industry in the third, and apparently by building construction in the fourth.[5] The basic proportions for aggregate production are thus determined by the choice of these focal points. All available information gives the impression that general political organizational goals constitute the primary influence over the plan directives, while the proportions of the various production programs by and large derive from rather arbitrary global coefficients of growth. The latter are then condensed, at the *Gosplan* stage, within the globally fixed proportions into concrete individual production goals.[6] It should be borne in mind that only such "proportions" and "general production goals" are suited for publication. Conceivably, the directives have been roughly weighed against each other, based on specific individual objectives.

The derivation of production goals for consumers' goods industries can be examined with more precision. Here, the central point of planning is the balancing of the population's money receipts and its money expenditures. In part, the money receipts are ascertainable from the planned fixed amounts paid by the State, such as wages and salaries and incomes from compulsory deliveries to the State, and in part are estimated as receipts from collective farm markets and private handicrafts. The various anticipated expenditures of the population, which represent money income to the State, are derived from the demands for consumers' goods.[7] The balance of these expenditures with the available consumer goods output results from varying the volume of production and its distribution between the "market fund" and the "nonmarket fund" (for institutional need) as well as varying prices or incomes.[8] In making choices among these variants, the "composite financial plan of the socialist economy," i.e., the balanced aggregate of all planned financial transactions of the State, is considered.[9] Beyond that, bases for planning the composition of consumers' goods are found in continuous investigations of the relative turnover of individual goods and changes in composition of demand under the influence of changes in income. There is some attempt to determine the correlation between changes in income and shifts in demand over periods of time. In this, statistics as to household expenditures of workers, employees, and collective peasants at varying income levels are used, and at least some attention is given to varying demand elasticities.[10] To be sure, this branch of planning is still young, since even aggregate balancing of money income of the population and commodity supply emerged from the experimental stage only about 1940, and its development certainly was retarded by the war and postwar confusion. Hence, the practical significance of this segment of planning remains doubtful.[11]

However, the question of planning principles in the consumers' goods sector has only secondary significance for an understanding of the principles of Soviet over-all planning. The really significant planning decisions are in the sphere

of State purposes, and besides defense industries, decisions
as to concrete ways of industrial growth and as to large investment projects hold first place.[12] Yet, every decision in
the realm of production of producers' goods is only a preliminary decision in the sense that it attains meaning only
after a subsequent decision has resulted in the production
of some final product. Among these end products benefiting
from planned investment, future consumption of the
population certainly plays a role. However, the specific
aspects of industrialization are not derived from this source.
As far as can be ascertained, the chief guide to investment
policy is an emphasis on those producers' goods industries
which, although they are not yet aimed at promoting the
fulfillment of a definite end purpose, do create multiuse
production capacity. Insofar as any definite end purpose can
be observed, it lies primarily in strengthening national defense, i.e., in armament.[13]

This brings us to the question as to the *origin** of the
goals set for the investment program. The conclusion just
reached may be stated more precisely for this purpose: The
chief economic efforts, with the possible exception of armament, do not serve any present end purposes, whether of
public or private nature, but rather serve to promote long-
term economic development, i.e., the basis for industrialization, as well as the creation of the general prerequisites,
namely a high production capacity in multiuse means of
such production as steel, machine construction, and energy
of all sorts. As for the closer determination of developmental
goals, it can only be said that the fundamental tasks and the
general direction are given by the directives, while the
specific target capacities of individual concerns to be constructed are planned by balancing production and use of

* Italics supplied by editor of translation.

all intermediate products. Here, so to say, is the problem of the long-term aspect of balances, where production capacities that are fixed short-term balances (allowing for some variations in intensity and direction) largely become variables so that the given production bases will have many-sided possibilities of adaptation to production tasks. Thus long-term planning (for five-year or perspective plans) has greater possibilities than short-term planning or annual plans. As to the fundamental determination of goals and the choice of "equitably balanced" plans for their realization, nothing definite can be established here other than that indexes of the over-all technical structure of individual branches of industry appear to play a role, and this will be discussed later.[14] Whenever this question is raised, Soviet economists assert that the choice of production goals (here, investment purposes), in large as in small matters, is *politically** decided, and is not subject to any *economic** considerations.

Balances

The balances, in which production means and production goals are made to coincide, step by step, are considered the basic focal points of Soviet economic planning. The name "method of balances" has been given to this type of Soviet economic planning. Actually, the method of balances is merely a matter of comparing the producible quantities of every good, on the one hand, with the requisite means of production on the other hand. These means include processing of supplementary material and using power resources, the construction of installations, the private consumption of workers, as well as personal requirements of management. Such a comparison must be supplemented with

necessary balances of exports-imports and of inventory ac-
cumulation-liquidation.[15] It assures the availability of production prerequisites for every succeeding stage, as well as
the utilization of the output potential of each earlier stage,
thus bringing to light any bottlenecks within the complex
of balances. Balancing in this sense is an obvious necessity
in every type of planning worthy of the name. The rigorous
use of balances is understandable in the light of the history
of Russian planning, for balances are the great achievement
of the first two five-year plans. Until the middle of the
twenties, production decisions were made primarily by
*local** agencies or plant directors. The activities of the
central planning agencies were limited to drawing up
partial plans for individual industries or industrial
branches, which manifestly were not coordinated into an
over-all plan. Moreover, the first attempts at comprehensive
planning of over-all economic activity, i.e., the control
figures for 1925-26 and 1926-27, apparently were only an
assembling of production goals of individual industries.
These were determined by extrapolating for each industry
from its current production development or were derived
from statistically determined and generally valid economic
proportions of earlier times, but were not balanced with
a view to achieving complete complementarity or coordination. Only the discovery, in the course of preliminary work
for the first Five-Year Plan (1928), of disproportionalities
in the development of various economic branches led to the
thought of using balancing. Even thereafter, balances were
drawn up for only a few of the most important industrial
branches and materials, and were not coordinated into a
system of balances. A process of increased refinement of
method followed. The number of economic branches in-

* Italics supplied by editor of translation.

cluded was enlarged, the interpretation of facts was refined, and the degree of possible mutual coordination of individual balances enhanced. The preparatory work for the second Five-Year Plan (1933) and the formation of functional divisions in *Gosplan* (which formerly had only industry branches) in 1935 are stages in this evolution.[16] Even now, while *Gosplan* prepares material balances for a large segment of products, the scope of the balances is still limited. It pertains to industries producing goods (funded products) that are allocated on the basis of a centralized allocation plan authorized by the Council of Ministers of the Union, and specifies the recipients and their requisite quantities. In 1950 such goods included over 1,500 items.[17] As to certain other categories of goods (quota products), the particular ministries, which are the chief producers of each good in question, draw up the balances. As for the remaining categories (the decentralized fund) there is apparently no over-all balancing. For them planning initiative appears to rest largely with regional and local organs of government, while the comprehensive plan of the central authorities merely provides the perimeter and controls and records the result in aggregate form.[18] There are recent tendencies toward strengthening decentralization in this sense, by expanding the functions of the ministerial bureaucracy as well as of regional organs.[19]

Besides the balances named thus far—the material resource balances, the labor force balances, and the balance of money income and expenditure of the population—there are also (1) the cash balance of the State Bank, (2) the State budget, (3) the "combined financial plan of the socialist economy," and (4) the "balance of the national economy." The first three are purely financial in a technical sense; they do not regulate economic goal-setting, since they pertain solely to the *financial** implementation of given production tasks. The last has no ascertainable functional significance at all.[20]

Norms as Element, Combining Balances: Their Determination

In order to combine the separate items in the balances at various stages of production, to derive the producible quantity of a good from the balances of various components of its production possibilities and the need for the good from the balances of its various uses, a connecting link is necessary in order to coordinate the balances at all stages of production into a composite system. This link is provided by the "norms," or "technical-economic indexes." The technical indexes of concerns make possible establishing the extent of production of individual factors, namely, of output capacities, of raw materials, of equipment, of fuel, and of electric power. The technical economic indexes are likewise the link between the separate sections of the plan and between the various phases of reproduction. The technical economic indexes of the equipment of enterprises establish the degree to which their available capacities are being exploited and thereby indicate what new capacities must be provided to fulfill the prescribed output program. They thus serve as a link between the production plan and the construction plan. Index numbers of consumption of raw material, fuel, equipment, and electric power represent the connection in planning between the complementary branches of socialized production: for example, the connection between the metal and oil industries on the one hand and the smelting industry on the other; between the

* Italics supplied by editor of translation.

smelting industry and machine construction; between light industry and the foodstuffs industry and agriculture.[21]

These norms are thus by nature ratios between the magnitudes of input items and the magnitudes of output results achieved, both expressed, as a rule, in physical units. Production input is occasionally indicated only partially by these indexes, in contrast with cost indexes, since the realization of a production result probably requires the use of several qualitatively different items of input for each of which an index number must be ascertained. Arithmetically these index numbers appear in two forms, either as input items or as output items in the denominator (the one is the reciprocal value of the other). We may call the former output norm (output per unit of input, also called "exploitation norm"), and the latter input norm (input per unit of output, also called "consumption norm"). According to the purpose of norming, these may be divided into three large groups: First, norms for the input of separate raw and supplementary materials, including energy per unit of product, or for the yield in finished products or semifabricated items per unit of raw material:[22] Second, norms for utilizing machines and plants; in general these appear as output norms (possible production achievement per machine unit); and they are then designated capacity norms. Besides these, input norms also occur (labor hour time per product), which, moreover, are distinguished as to whether the capacity has been technically fixed in relation to the physical equipment of the plant (for example, the volume of its boilers or ovens), or whether it is dependent on a varying degree of utilization of this stated capacity, etc.[23] Finally, in the third place, norms for the utilization of labor usually appear as input norms (labor input time per unit of product). In the form of output norms they can be combined mathematically with labor productivity, but the latter apparently are used more for aggregate control purposes than for specific determination of labor requirement.[24]

The methods of computing norms are important. To understand the problem they pose, reference must be made to the hybrid nature of the norms. Norms form the basis for setting production programs of all industrial branches and of individual enterprises, as well as the relevant allocation plans for initial and intermediate products. They thus serve as neutral checks of these varied production programs, since the several enterprises and industrial branches are necessarily related as providers and receivers of the initial and intermediate products. Indeed, they are intended to establish a relationship among the production programs so that they fit together without surpluses or deficits. This requires that consumption coefficients, exploitation coefficients, and capacity coefficients are taken into account that are subsequently actually attained. Utilization of too favorable coefficients would mean that the output result is too low because of inadequate availability of the input factor, whose exploitation was estimated too favorably. In consequence, those production programs based on this output result, required by them as working capital, likewise suffer. Finally, the remaining input components as well as their output, as such, and also subsequently dependent outputs whose exploitation was not estimated as favorably, appear as surplus and therefore are not usable. At the same time, the norms determine in general the achievements required of plants and workers. The produced achievement is scarcely ever higher but is frequently lower than that which is required. Stepping up of achievement, continuously more thrifty operation with materials, ever better utilization of establishments and labor power, can be accomplished only by stepping up the requirements represented by the norms. One is thus faced with the dilemma either of a stagnation of the economic productivity relationships or an inadequate coordination of the economic efforts, with resultant misdirection and consequent waste of economic productive power.[25]

Initially norms were apparently arrived at by assembling statistically the actually realized values of the several operations and computing their averages. During the middle of the thirties it was recognized that norms had possibilities as starting points for the planned development of productivity, serving particularly as means for systematic control and stimulation of economic activity of management and of laborers. Thus the propaganda campaign began to displace the so-called statistical or arithmetical average norms by progressive average norms. The latter are an average value between the general average norm and the maximum values realized by individual best workers and by best enterprises. While for individual achievements input norms are lowered according to plan or output norms are raised, the same production components (materials, establishments, labor power) yield an ever-increasing performance, and so stimulate economic productivity. Recently this method has been increasingly criticized insofar as it represents the schematic computation of an average above the average of the output figures. At the same time, the "technically established norms" appear in addition to the progressive average norms. These are ascertained by research and computations as to the technically possible degree of achievement and utilization. For labor accomplishments, such norms are established through labor time studies.[26]

The transition to "progressive average norms" and "technically established norms" is by no means completed. Actually the "arithmetically averaged norms" or "empirical-statistical norms" continue to play an important role in planning practice.[27] Perhaps the reasons for this are the inertia of the managerial apparatus, addicted as it is to an established methodology, and the fact that the routine handling of the empirical-statistical method is easier and therefore appears to be better suited for application within a managerial framework. Moreover, it must also be considered that since the beginning of the campaign no incentive existed to stimulate the systematic development of planning methods. The immediate interests of preparation for war, the conduct of the war, and reconstruction demanded the energies of the managerial apparatus for a long time. The previously mentioned schism in real interests may also play a part. For its purposes, the managerial apparatus has to be more interested in mutual harmonizing of the activities of individual establishments and in the computation of realistically consistent input and output indexes than in stimulating new planning methods. For these reasons, the empirical-statistical method is more suitable for it.

Norms as Routine Stimulation of the Economy

There are instances where the method of progressive norm setting has found a form that has routine applicability. Conceptually, progressive movement of norms rests on the generalization of such improvements of production methods as have been discovered and tested only at particular points, but are realizable everywhere in like manner. Progressive norm-setting is intended to force the general introduction of these improvements and make them useful in planning results. The accomplishments of the Stakhanov workers are not always actual proof of the prevalence of such generally applicable improvements, since they frequently have come about as a result of favorable, exceptional conditions or the application of greater physical energy or mental concentration, which cannot be employed continuously. Where this is the case, concerns are confronted with problems pertaining to the relation of input and output, the solution of which cannot be clearly indicated by the planner.[28] Concerns have to accomplish an increase in achievement, a lowering of expenditures, in one way or another. On the basis of available material, only conjectures are possible as to whether, beyond this, improvements of norms that might take the form of aggregative decreed coefficients for increased productivity are planned, while changes in and direction of individual norms take place by making these initial aggregate norms specific.[29] The centrally set norms as starting points of planning must certainly produce a tendency in this direction. This method of making economic progress by orderly directing of procedure in discovering and observing opportunities, which has a certain commercial-speculative appearance, may be contrasted with the bureaucratic method. It can obviously never be fully realized, since the components of productivity that may be arbitrarily established are limited, and any additional realized increase in productivity remains dependent on finding unbiased possibilities. Bureaucratic tendencies must necessarily appear in an economic system in which responsibility for economic progress depends primarily on the energies of the central agencies.[30]

This method has its counterpart in the field of investment planning. Besides the norms just considered serving as combination of balances and measurement of performance, a second large group appears as indexes of over-all technical structure of an industrial branch or a type of production.

This includes "indexes of the optimal equipment of a concern" or of "the best condition of the finishing process," which show the share of this branch in the total capacity, ascribed to the plants using the most modern production methods or the most modern construction, as well as the "indexes of mechanization of labor intensive processes," focusing particular attention on the relation between manual labor and mechanical labor in successive stages of production. In addition, the input and output norms play a role in this group in that the scattering of practically realized values by an industrial branch (or type of production) reveals the expansion and development possibilities of the aggregate technical structure of this branch.[31] The indexes of this second group apparently form an essential basis for directing investment for long-term development plans of individual branches of industry, so that a certain degree of technical modernization is considered necessary for individual industrial branches, depending on their importance in the framework of over-all goal-setting. Thus a criterion for investment guidance is attained, permitting a clear conception of the nature of the decision made, and differing typically from the effectiveness criterion of our theory (capital yield). Indeed, a certain intellectual relationship will be established with the corresponding components of the contrasting pairs of norms previously described. Whereas the commercial-speculative method of investment planning familiarizes itself with the many opportunities for economizing and gain-sharing, extending irregularly over the entire field of production decisions, the bureaucratic method tends toward a systematic, piecemeal procedure, so that in operating sectors there will be an all-embracing use of means, without considering the comparable individual advantage attainable from every minute input. The discussion of the effectiveness criterion in the Soviet Union in recent years indicates that investment planning in the Soviet Union does not proceed solely according to this principle.[32] Its primary meaning derives from the weight assigned to index numbers of the second group, and particularly from the way the issue of "mechanizing" labor-intensive-processes is viewed. The slogan is "complex mechanization," i.e., in reconstructing or modernizing concerns and branches of production, all types of manual labor shall as far as possible be replaced by machines and later by automation in all successive intermediate stages of the production process.[33]

Participation of Central and Lower Agencies in Drawing Up of the Plan

One further distinction between norms is significant. This is between individual norms and aggregative norms. Thus Zacharov and Oligin distinguish all-union (interbranch), branch, and enterprise norms.[34] As to their relation to each other, D'jačenko states: "Branch or aggregate economic norms differ among enterprises, depending on the labor conditions of every individual concern. For some of the most progressive enterprises, input norms are set lower than branch norms. This means lower than the planned level of socially necessary outlay for producing goods of a particular type. In other enterprises which lag in technique and organization of production, they are set higher than branch norms." [35] Grunkin reports that the function of technical norming in the plant consists of "unraveling and differentiating" the "average progressive directive norms" handed down from higher up, which are "aggregative crude norms," because precise and concrete norms are necessary within each division and for operative labor of the plant, while norms for labor input and raw material use, for example, are as a rule given for total product; performance norms are given for groups of machines.[36]

The actual meaning of this differentiation becomes apparent when one considers the possible participation of the higher and lower stages of the planning and management apparatus in drawing up the plan, and when one raises the question as to the position of this apparatus, which combines the separate items of the various balances with the aid of the norms. With the discussion of this question, the presentation of the method of balances is necessarily completed and rounded out.

The following dilemma now arises: On the one hand, norms serving as the bases for computing individual input and output items change from enterprise to enterprise, owing to varying conditions of production and output scarcity. The accounting procedure for determining the requisite input items necessary to fulfill definite production tasks or the output obtainable with the available production means is, in itself, as many-sided as the production process in industry. Therefore, the planning apparatus of the industrial organization structure must either be broken down into detail or the entire managerial apparatus must be tied to the planning process. On the other hand, the one element, the requisite output quantity or the available production basis, is not given in any of the calculations as unilaterally determinable, for the requisite or possible size of both elements for every single computation is, in turn, dependent on the parallel computations for every other industrial basic unit that uses the products or furnishes preliminary products. Determination of planned tasks, which is the prerequisite for computing the relevant input items, presupposes knowledge of them. It is also impossible to develop the entire computation process from one end, namely either the objectives to be realized or the available final production means and the direction of their use, and thus to establish successively for every computed individual process an item as starting point. Moreover, the objectives to be realized and the direction of use of final production means are mutually determinable only in the course of the planning process, as alternative possibilities become apparent, since in the allocation procedure various goods are mutually interchangeable intermediary products ("backward substitution"). All individual items in planning computation are simultaneously interchangeable determinants. Yet all quantities must be determined at the same time in striking the balance for the entire process. Carrying out such balancing of alternatively determinate magnitudes naturally requires repeated variation of individual items. Obviously this cannot be accomplished by computing with the previously indicated polynomial.

It thus follows that determination of balanced production requirements, embracing the entire economy, cannot take into account all separate items, but is limited to global quantities of individual products and types of products. Specifically, relations between input and output items that are established by making decisions for the entire economy cannot depend on a calculation of the requisite means for a unit of product or (vice versa) on the basis of a previous computation with the aid of a relevant aggregative norm. The draft of the plan drawn up with the aid of lump-sum norms must naturally be particularized by distributing computed planned tasks and input quantities among industrial entities set up anew as individual norms for separate enterprises and made more precise than is possible with crude aggregate norms The refined individual results thus attained once more require subsequent coordination.

The picture generally presented of the origin of the plan of the Soviet Union coincides with conclusions reached here. It may be described as follows: based on the directives given by the Party (the Central Committee) and the Government (Council of Ministers), *Gosplan* works out the draft of a plan.[37] This is then passed downward by the managerial hierarchy and continuously made more specific: on the one hand by Union ministries, chief administrative agencies, and trusts, to centrally managed enterprises. Similarly, by *Gosplans* of the republics and by Union ministries and Republic ministries of the Union, it is passed down to enterprises managed by the republics. On the other hand, it is passed down by the planning commissions of the republics, territories (*oblasts*), districts (*rajon*), and cities to locally managed enterprises. It is studied in the enterprises; suggestions are made for changes; and then the hierarchy is retraced upward where, in each stage, altered data are made to balance anew. On the basis of this progressively developed draft of the plan, *Gosplan* draws up the final plan after completing a last coordination. It is then ratified by the Council of Ministers, thus becoming law, and as a legal obligation again descends through the managerial hierarchy to the individual enterprises.[38]

The detailed number of quantities involved in drawing up the draft of the plan naturally can be measured in various ways. The larger it is, the more comprehensive is the apparatus that participates in this initial labor. The more cumbersome and drawn out it becomes in order to bring about variations in individual magnitudes, the more difficult it becomes to survey the alternatives and the less likely it is that the production means and given objectives will be combined consistently in a definite sequence, aimed at their attainment. In place of conscious formation of proportions for the entire plan, the connection must be made more and more with an incidental starting point, namely the existing program, where the prevailing directives of use of production means appear and the balance likewise thus becomes merely a subsequent correction to remove obvious inconsistencies.

Russian economic planning evidently has long since surpassed the above described method. Originally, concrete formulation of the plan began with the lower planning agencies. These were influenced only by general lines of action, "directives" in the actual sense, in order to stimulate further development from a static starting point, i.e., to expand the existing program in a definite direction. The function of *Gosplan* was primarily in the sphere of subsequent coordination. Even the method of balances initially served only this purpose.[39] The transition to the method of planning here presented appears to have been made[40] primarily in the year 1938 when, for the first time, the setting up of the most important balances was preceded by the insertion of ministries[41] into the drawing up of the plan. Further evidence of present procedure as well as of recent development in drawing up of a preliminary comprehensive draft of the plan with the aid of aggregative norms is found in Lokšin.[42] This pertains to the number of material input norms used in setting up plans for state needs, particularly in comparison with the data as to goods balances (cited above) on the one hand and with the number of norms in individual concerns on the other hand. In drawing up the plan for 1949, some 1,800 material input norms were used. For the 1950 plan, this figure had become over 4,500, and, for the 1951 plan, more than 6,000.

--✦ 2 ✦--

The Place of Financial Planning
in the Soviet Planning System

The Economic Sense of Money Calculation

A GUIDED economic system is conceivable in which the previously described *quantity* planning would suffice. At least theoretically, it is adequate to determine the extent and direction of economic activity. Ideas of purely material planning, with the abolition of monetary calculations, together with a somewhat vague notion of substituting labor-hour reckoning, actually played an important role in early Marxism and Bolshevism. Even today they represent the ultimate goal of Communism. Discovering and establishing the necessity for monetary calculations in the present stage of socialism is lauded as the particular achievement of Stalin.[1]

The real significance of financial planning[2] and monetary calculation is as follows: it makes possible a logical solution of the problem of economic choice, insofar as economic decisions of individuals (choices) are related to the idea of achieving realizable over-all maximum or optimum want satisfaction, combined quantitatively into a corresponding consistent relationship. This problem cannot be solved within the framework of purely material planning, because it requires that the variable conditions for realizing the final material objectives of individuals, i.e., the allocation of "economic resources" ("goods of a higher order") to attain or not to attain various objectives, shall proceed in such manner that the goods chosen will yield to those making the choices the maximum satisfaction obtainable from the available productive resources. To achieve such allocation, the input of economic means must be so distributed among its alternative uses that every unit will yield maximum material want satisfaction, and will be directed to that use where output will be largest. Such decisions presuppose a knowledge of the significance ascribed to interrelated individual material purposes. Except perhaps in a "Robinson Crusoe economy" or at least in a small closed economy or self-sufficient economy, such decisions ordinarily are not made by a single head, undertaking the determination of relevant aggregate relationships of final goals. Hence, qualitatively different and noncomparable material goods must be expressed in terms of a common unit of measurement.[3] Economic means must also be included in this valuation, with the aid of a common unit of measurement since, as intermediate products, they are again to a large extent the results of economic efforts. These, in turn, require the utilization of economic resources to make them available and thus appear in their allocation among various possible uses as competitive alternatives as well as final goals. Their evaluation must proceed according to the significance they bear to realizing individual goals and hence to aggregate want satisfaction. Their value is thus derived from that of the final goal. In this manner an over-all value system is constructed. It values all individual economic aims and means, relative to maximum fulfillment of purpose, and integrates them into a closed, purely quantitative or numerical set of relationships.[4]

Such a conceptual relationship is established by monetary calculations, insofar as the value system functions consistently. Thus the value of a good (of first or higher order) becomes the directive. It indicates the importance attached to this good among the intermediate and final production goals, and directs a corresponding portion of total economic expenditures or aggregate productive effort into its production. It is to be observed, however, that money value as a directive is in this sense only a derived criterion whose magnitude is explained by the composition and priority of the desired assortment of end products and the importance of the evaluated goods needed to realize them. Hence, it exercises its directive influence only in the sense of indicating final purposes. Since this final assortment of purposes that determines the entire value system is material, the whole process of choosing can conceptually be conceived of as in kind. It is realizable, however, only with the aid of a valuation system, since only this makes the actual alternatives visible among all elements of the economic process. One might say that making valuation is identical with choosing. But, in any event, money evaluation in the service of economic choice is purely instrumental. The function performed by money as the instrument of economic choice might be called *evidence function*. Money makes evident the over-all significance of individual purposes and of means for economic fulfillment of purpose and thus facilitates consistent economic choice.

It is particularly important for the trend of thought in this study to state that a purely formal function is dealt with here. This function is independent of the source of objectives that are weighed against each other as to their relative importance. Even today there is a certain inclination to identify the effectiveness of the price system with subordination of the economy to the goals of the private consumer. This identification was found necessary for the modern price theory, because of its subjective, psychological beginning. But actually such identification is not justified. Moreover, besides the influence of private consumers there is in all present-day price systems a public demand for fulfilling collective goals. If, for example, a public agency needs copper to complete its aircraft construction program, so that copper becomes scarce and its price rises, this is no distortion of the price system by noneconomic influences. Objectively, this product actually has become scarcer and more sought for, and hence is more valuable. In like manner a price system may be conceived that consists entirely of state value judgments and goal-setting.

The assumptions as to the applicability and usefulness of our price theory are as follows:

1. A many-sided, graduated system of economic goals must be given, whose order of rank is not absolute but is to a certain extent at least dependent on how far one goal must be sacrificed in order to realize another determinate goal, i.e., on the existing exchange relationships among individual final objectives.

2. The attainability of these objectives must depend on the use of a likewise diversified but generally scarce supply of intermediate products, whose unit quantities may be combined for various purposes in varying amounts.

3. Finally, price theory is of particular significance if and

to the extent that there are substitution possibilities among
the various means, with changing substitution relationships.
Accordingly, individual unit quantities of goods attain
varying significance for fulfillment of purposes, based on the
extent of their use in combination with other means, and
the law of variable proportions becomes operative.

The price system is thus understood as the mere instrument to realize the most effective use of the available
economic means to attain set goals, regardless of their origin.
It is also devoid of every ethical condemnation or justification. It is, rather, subjected to only a quasi-technical judgment, and is relieved of every limitation as to its applicability set by particular historical or ideological systems.[5,6]

The particular difficulty posed by the consideration of the
place of financial planning in the Soviet directed economic
system arises from the attitudes toward the insertion of
money in this its primary economic function—its evidence
function—which is said to be contradictory in itself. This
is denied, basically. Primarily, there is a misunderstanding of
the role played by financial valuation indexes of purposes
and means within the framework of directed production,
and particularly in determining production goals. It is
concluded that from its function as leading criteria and
particularly from the role assigned to profit margins—
"profitability" in the formation of the value system—that
the effects of financial valuation are not limited to the significance of making evident economic elements within the
framework and on the basis of given aggregate economic
goal-setting, but that money and money value can also
exercise an automatic directive function in guiding economic effort, contrary to this suggested goal-setting. It is
primarily the conception of a short-sighted, momentary
interest of consumers, which might become apparent in this

manner, contrary to plan. We thus arrive at the meaningless alternative of a planning system explainable in terms of particular monetary circumstances in the developmental stage but a consistently developed economic value system—assuming correct understanding of the role of financial criteria, i.e., profitability or material goal-setting, according to plan—which is then naturally decided in favor of the plan.

This rejection of the evidence function of money, the directive characteristics of financial value magnitudes, cannot be carried out consistently. In the first place, one does not want to abandon the use of money accounting and financial planning for other reasons. But every use of money accounting and of money magnitudes produces certain secondary effects, which automatically and unavoidably makes it a directive criterion. This is the point of departure in this presentation. Beyond that, however, in a certain sense use is naïvely made of money quantities that attain meaning only if they are intended as elements of a consistent economic value system. They are employed in a certain respect, within limits, as directive criteria from the outset, without explanation.

The Introduction of Money Calculation for Control of Plan

The point from which the need for money accounting arises in the Soviet planning system is the need for control of plan fulfillment, and thence, in general, the performance of workers. This might be called a developmental and control function of money, in contrast with the evidence function.[7] On the one hand, the economic control measures are intended to assure that the lower producing economic

units, the "enterprises," fulfill their production tasks
quantitatively and qualitatively but that on the other hand
they remain within the limits of the prescribed use of various input items per unit of product. It is immediately apparent that such control is inconceivable in material units, if
one considers on the one hand the multiplicity of produced
goods and, on the other, the required number of input
items for the output of a good, in addition to the many
requisite outlays for simultaneous products. The many-sided-
ness of the products and the appearance of quality of performance become apparent only with further processing.
Even the mere comprehension of input and output performances of an enterprise would be complex, particularly
the accounting control for adherence to prescribed input
norms. If at all, it could be carried out only by an apparatus
so extensive that it could recapitulate every single economic
movement within an enterprise, and then not continuously,
but only for longer intervals. Furthermore, such a material
control would produce a mixture of shortage and surplus
items, but would give no picture of the total performance
of the enterprise. This is because discrepancies in performance are unavoidable and their causes are partly beyond
the responsibility of the enterprise, lying in the realm of
delivered and intermediate products. Finally, the question
arises as to the controlling agency and the supervision or
association of interests: Who shall take care of the custodian?
Based on experience, the obviously responsible, immediately
superior authority is of limited use only, since it is jointly
responsible for revealed losses. A certain assurance of
control can be attained here only insofar as the losses are
also observable by the next higher agency. An independently
created control apparatus will be more harmful than useful
because of lack of clarity of subordinate relationship, as

well as because of frictions and jealousies. The reliability of the work of such a control, not entrusted with an independently functioning and decision-making apparatus, will likewise remain questionable, quite apart from the costliness of such a dual apparatus. To establish mutual control by selling and buying enterprises would be fruitful only insofar as these enterprises are interested in such control because of their main function and responsibility, namely, their production task.

Actually, all the material controls are built into the Soviet directing apparatus that could be supplied with reasonable managerial effort. The progress of plan fulfillment is supervised by specific divisions and officials of the planning commission, aided by statistical reports of enterprises.[9] In particular, the allocation of products at all stages is centralized to the fullest extent. A particular system of divisions of sale and purchase has been established, subordinate to the ministries and chief administrative agencies, to plan, control and, as far as possible, carry out the plan. In some respects, delivery relationships have the appearance of allocation by the superior authority and delivery to it. However, this could not be done for all goods; for the less important items the system had to be broken down into two stages, the lower one permitting the enterprises to make a rather free search for supply and demand opportunities.[10]

For goods in the upper two stages whose distribution is centrally directed, it was also impossible to dispense with the cooperative control of enterprises of the same rank, as buyers and sellers, or of other enterprising agencies. Here a peculiar mixed system is used, both in formulating the planned task and in controlling its execution, which combines "legal managerial" orders and individual "civil law" obligations. Developing turnover of output produced according to plan proceeds in accordance with the so-called "civil law" contracts between enterprises. However, the plan determines the volume of output, though possibly only in the aggregate, depending on the nature of the product, and the contracting parties. The contract is said to specify the planned task in detail by closer examination of "assortment," i.e., quality, precise quantity, and other variable details as to the goods to be delivered and by establishing exact terms of delivery. This double-tracked form is not chosen to delimit an area in which enterprises may shape output freely, according to their own judgment. It is rather a matter of interest for control of planned activity to achieve advance obligatory regulation of those production details that can be regulated effectively only by the participating parties. Contracts thus are merely a necessary supplement to give precision to the plans. Consequently, entering into such arrangements is an obligation of the participants.[11]

Observance of the prescribed output volume according to plan and its distribution by means of the material control system are not assured. This is apparent from the numerous complaints as to changes of the production program contrary to plan,[12] particularly nonadherence to the assortment plan and the accumulation of raw materials[13] in violation of plan. Moreover, the related attempts to exercise influence on the pertinent behavior of enterprises by corresponding manipulation of prices and profit margins would be meaningless if the material control system were effective.[14]

It is essential for our trend of thought that inserting of enterprises for mutual control of performance, which becomes unavoidable by permitting direct task relationships between them, necessarily introduces financial elements into the directed economic system. Effective mutual control can be achieved only if the regular exercise of control activity is a condition for the fulfillment of the main task by which the performance of the enterprise is judged and where, therefore, a neglect of the problem of control would appear as a deficiency of production. In order to accomplish this, the economic connection between the performance of one enterprise and the input item of another must be made apparent in the practice of controlling performance; the recipient may relieve the controlled enterprise of its performance responsibility only by permitting himself to be credited with an input of the same magnitude, and thus assuming responsibility for the composition and maintenance of the value of this performance, as though it were of his own output. This actual assumption of performance and responsibility presupposes a common medium in which the performance of both enterprises, the provider and the recipient, can be expressed, including the many possible forms of deficiency in performance such as late delivery, deviation of quality, style, and assortment. Successful mutual output control of enterprises is thus possible only by introducing a general medium of exchange and making payment for received services in this exchange medium. In this way a financial relationship is established throughout the entire economy, which makes feasible pursuing the progress of each economic task from one production stage to another through all the appearing and again disappearing specific material stages, until the final destination is reached (consumption, fulfillment of final purposes, "use"), and supervising its attainment.

The second reason why money accounting is unavoidable, solely for purposes of control, is thus indicated. In order to be able to distinguish at a glance among the multiplicity of enterprises those that make intervention necessary because of inadequate performance from those that because of occasional—actually unavoidable—output difficulties, but which nevertheless generally operate satisfactorily, the confusing complexity of individual material items must be made apparent to the controlling eye. The many-sided deficit and surplus outputs resulting from the economic activity of the enterprise, at times with one offsetting the other, must be combined in a uniform aggregate performance. This again requires a common medium, this time purely calculable: ". . . for the results of the whole economic performance of an enterprise can never be expressed in material units—and compared with the results of individual concerns and branches of the economy." [15]

This also holds true if the economic task is considered merely technical, as realizable planned data, where it is solely a matter of adherence or nonadherence to plan. However, performance is not such a technical datum; it varies, depending on the efforts of the workers. It can be increased and in Russian economic planning, as we saw in the first chapter, special emphasis is placed on this dynamic aspect, on this possibility of realizing increased output. To be sure, this pertains directly to specific individual material achievements only, measured in terms of norms. However, if stimulation of initiative and of systematic increase in performance is sought, so that it becomes a significant force in economic life, the aggregate output of every economic unit must be made apparent. This makes it particularly necessary to combine all individual performances—abstract, i.e., financial—into an aggregate achievement, thus permitting the comparison of performances of various units, as well as determining a relationship between achievement and compensation of the worker, both of which are of particular significance as stimuli to the will to work.

Here is the chief point for the method of financial planning that has been developed in the Soviet Union since the end of the twenties, and under the term *khozraschet*[16] has become one of the most widely discussed subjects of economic propaganda. "Realization of *khozraschet* is based on the conscious, planned use of the law of value, modified, in form, by the Soviet State. In order to know how much the work of every enterprise costs, in order to be able to compare outlays and results of the activity of the enterprise constantly, a *common measure** is necessary which makes possible reducing all outlays of enterprises to a common denominator. This common denominator is Soviet money, with the aid of which an exact monetary accounting of receipts and expenditures of an enterprise is brought about." [17] The performance of an enterprise is thus expressed as the difference between income and outgo, as either surplus or deficit in money receipts, as profit or loss. Depending on the importance attached to attaining overfulfillment of plan, operating without loss is not merely a preliminary indicator of abiding by the prescribed input norms of the plan. Realized profit is also significant as an expression of positive achievement of an enterprise. Thus it has become possible to develop *khozraschet,* which initially was a means of financial control of the plan, into a regular "profitability" system. It is therefore defined as "a Soviet method of managing an enterprise so that the proceeds from the sale of products cover all outlays and in addition assure a saving." [18]

Particular attention has been given in Soviet literature to the problem of determining the relation between performance and compensation. This problem would appear to create particular difficulty because of the Communist ideal, related to economic dogma in general. Its treatment indi-

* Italics supplied by editor of translation.

cates how freely, at times, one plays around with transmitted doctrines if they conflict with the interests of practical economic guidance. The catchword that deals with the question is the so-called "stimulus," the incentive that on the one hand moves the lower agencies of economic management and on the other the workers themselves to achieve the planned tasks, and in particular to strive to step up economic performance. Readiness to do so is not contained, as such, in the Socialist-Communist ideal, nor can it be aroused solely by education and appeal to the desire for social distinction.[19] It retains an unalterable relationship to the "material interests" of workers and hence a participation in the distribution of the social product.

> The reason for such independence of enterprises grows out of the nature of social labor in the Socialist stage, in which, although it ceases to be labor for the exploiter, becomes labor for the laborer himself, for his society. Nevertheless it has not yet become the primary requirement in man's life. Because of these circumstances, it becomes necessary to introduce the factor of personal-material interestedness in the organization of production, one of the decisive stimuli for the development of productive power. [To carry this out,] the Socialist principle of distribution according to performance establishes the material interest of the worker in his work, and furthermore creates the necessary conditions for correct coordination of personal and social interests.[20]

To establish such a relation between performance and compensation, a uniform medium in which performance and compensation can be expressed is again assumed, making possible financial cost accounting, *khozraschet,* and money payment (even, as previously indicated, for measuring the volume of output). "As long as there is no surplus production, wages in kind create conditions favoring the introduction of elements of equalization, which are in sharp contrast with the socialist principle of payment, according to deed. Out of commodity-money wage payment arises the possibility . . . of a consistent application of the socialist principle of payment according to deed. . . ." [21]

The tendency toward realizing this principle occurs, in the first place, in fixing wage relationships,[22] particularly in the system of profit-sharing of enterprises and workers, closely related to the concept *khozraschet*. "Planned profitability of every enterprise is said to be at a level sufficient to interest the enterprise in the financial results of its activity, i.e., . . . secondly, to yield deductions in favor of the Director's Fund, which can serve as incentive to increase labor productivity, and to improve the organization of the entire production process." [23] The system developed initially, in that the ability of management of an enterprise to pay premiums, to improve collective living standards of employees (kindergartens, clubs, recreation homes, workers' homes), as well as labor effectiveness (by quasi-investments for which management of the enterprise assumed responsibility), was made dependent on the extent of managerial initiative by allocating a part of planned and unplanned profits, i.e., financial surplus above costs, to a special fund for these purposes (since 1936 called the "Director's Fund").[24] The immediate beneficiary (in the Fund), the extent of which was determined in advance, was the management of the enterprise, whose position and reputation among personnel as well as whose operational efficiency were directly dependent on the successful operation of the enterprise.[25] The personnel was only indirectly interested in decisions of management, and therefore in no calculable manner. However, now the effort is made increasingly to

establish a direct relationship between individual performance of employees and workers and the size of the premiums,
so that automatically a definite percentage of a saved sum
(namely of lowered operating expenses) accrues to him who
achieves it.[26] Typically, with further development of the
premium system, the focal point of interest is the leading
employee, whether in the sphere of accounting, management,
or engineering; therefore it is he upon whose work method
the success of the enterprise largely depends.[27]

The introduction of profit and financial behavior in the
system of economic control creates not only a new criterion
for the economic conduct of enterprises but also creates the
opportunity for introducing further control agencies such
as the banking system. It is likewise reflected in a much-
used catch phrase, ruble control.

> In connection herewith, particular significance attaches to
> the systematic control of the progress in fulfilling produc-
> tion and commodity circulation plans, and the orderly
> utilization of materials allotted to enterprises by state
> agencies, particularly by the finance and credit system.
> Short-term credit granted by *Gosbank* (State Bank) plays
> an important role in strengthening *khozraschet*. Credit
> assures mobilization of money reserves of the State, for
> planned circulation of means of economic organizations, in
> the interest of plan fulfillment. On the credit basis, *Gosplan*
> conducts daily ruble control over the work of economic
> organizations.[28]

To carry out these controls, the bank is authorized, in general, to keep accounts. For aggregate payment transactions
of an enterprise, a branch office (of the bank) is the sole
custodian of accounts, and from time to time this bank provides the requisite cash sums needed for wage payments. In

this way it can supervise the aggregate financial conduct of enterprises indebted to it. In particular, the bank controls the planned economic activity of enterprises as a result of granting credit. Credits may be granted only in accordance with the need for fulfilling planned tasks, and only as quotas, according to periods of need. The return flow of credits is an indication of the corresponding progress of plan fulfillment by the debtor enterprise, since it must be derived from the proceeds of planned production. In order to subject enterprises to this control, it is necessary that only a part of their requirement for funds be met with their own working capital. Thereby they are made dependent on bank credit to finance their production. At the same time, there is an attempt to subject the branch offices of the bank to a certain pressure in fulfilling their control obligation. This is done by requiring that at least cash receipts and expenditures are so balanced in the cash plan of *Gosbank* that the branch offices must press for prompt inflow of receipts and corresponding plan fulfillment, primarily in retail trade, in order to be able to meet planned demands on them, particularly by enterprises to meet wage payments.[29]

Attempts are also made to use the tax system, specifically the turnover tax and the profits tax, for control purposes.

Turnover tax revenue is fundamentally dependent on the volume of produced and realized industrial and agricultural output, combined in large measure with the quality of the produced goods, insofar as this affects the rate of turnover of these goods. . . . Collection of the turnover tax thus becomes an essential means of control over the progress in plan fulfillment of production enterprises and trading organizatons. Nonfulfillment of the revenue plans drawn up for the turnover tax may indicate deviations from the output or sales plans for individual types of goods, due to defective work of enterprises or of the trade network. It may also indicate clearing difficulties, representing anomalies of one kind or another in economic-financial practices, or violation of financial discipline on the part of the taxpayers. In all such cases, the finance agencies must inquire whether the measures which assure fulfillment of the plan have been met. . . . Since the State budget of the USSR receives a part of money accumulations of the economy in the form of profit deductions, it exercises ruble control over the formation of profits by enterprises. A significant role in exercising this control relates to the examination of drafts of income and outgo balances, in drawing up the budget and analyzing monthly-quarter and annual-balance sheets of enterprises and Ministries.[30]

To control them prior to the war, industrial branches producing capital goods, while theoretically exempt from the turnover and the profits tax, paid at least minimum rates.[31] But this has been changed since the war.[32]

The Differing Attitude Toward Use of Financial Magnitudes as Lead Criteria

The system of financial planning is intended solely as such a control system to serve the material plan.

The most important indicator of the correctness of the ways and methods of strengthening *khozraschet* is assuring maximum success in fulfilling and overfulfilling the plans set by the State, by better use of material-, labor-, and money-reserves. . . . Every non-fulfillment of planned tasks, both quantitatively and qualitatively, every excess in planned norms of expenditure, with correct organization of the enterprise, worsens its financial economic position, on the basis of *khozraschet,* and disturbs punctual and adequate provision of means for all its current needs. Dependence of the financial economic conditions of an enterprise on the degree of fulfillment of planned tasks, on quality and results of its activity, is also the basis of ruble control, combined with *khozraschet*.[33]

In socialist enterprises the size of the profit depends on how the production program and the problem of lowering prime costs are solved . . . *khozraschet* aims at strict adherence to planned assortment of products and systematic improvement of quality. . . .[34] "The State plan is the first principle of *khozraschet*. Planned tasks as to quantity and variety of products, lower production costs, introduction of new techniques, etc., are the actual starting point for the organization of production within the enterprise." [35]

Accordingly, money magnitudes as lead criteria and "profitability viewpoint" as the determinant of production goals are rejected.

By the method of *khozraschet* the Soviet State itself sets the goal, to make all enterprises profitable, and to increase their profitability. However, the Soviet State is not guided by the quest for maximum profit. Rather, it is the principles of socialistic expanded reproduction which assure economic independence, indivisible supremacy of the socialist economic system, and strengthening of national defense. In deciding questions of creating and developing enterprises and industrial branches, the Soviet State is guided by their significance for socialist construction, regardless of their profitability. If, for example, in a certain stage of its development, a heavy industry enterprise does not yield a profit, but is of major importance for the economy as a whole, it will nevertheless be constructed. . . . On the basis of the planning system all necessary industrial branches are developed, regardless of their direct, immediate profitability.[36]

Prices and prime costs of individual products express the relation of expenditure of social labor in their production only in the most general terms. Nor does the accumulation formed in this or that branch of the economy indicate precisely the degree of labor productivity in this branch. Thus, in 1938, heavy industry yielded 16 per cent of the aggregate profits and turnover tax receipts, light and textile industry 22 per cent, while 50 per cent came from the food industries, etc. This certainly does not mean that labor expenditures were less productive in heavy industry, i.e., that a larger part of these expenditures was required for the simple replacement of used means of production and for wage payments of workers and employees, and that it contributed less to the socialist accumulation fund. The given relationship between accumulations in heavy and foodstuff industries merely indicates that in fixing the price level of industrial production, the Soviet State so distributes accumulation among branches of the economy that a larger part of liquid funds is made available for the sale of products in the foodstuff industries and a correspondingly smaller part in the sale of products of heavy industry.[37]

This question is currently being treated in Russia under the catch phrase: Role of the law of value under Socialism. Determination of production goals based on profit considerations is designated recognition of the law of value as "regulator of production." Such a regulatory role, however, is not ascribed to it. In this connection the discussion centers primarily around the controversy relating to the method of industrialization that was waged toward the end of the twenties. This had to do with whether light (consumer goods) or heavy (capital goods) industries should be given precedence,[38] where the question of light industry development becomes identical with gearing the economic goal to profit.

> The working of the law of value as regulator of production appears, above all, in the preferential development of those branches of production that are most profitable, that yield most gain, the largest return for every ruble spent or per unit of output. If the law of value plays the regulating role in production, materials, labor power, and financial means have to be directed primarily into these production branches. As for the less profitable branches of production, those that yield less gain, they must develop more slowly because of the regulatory effects of the law of value, or the scarcely profitable and especially the unprofitable concerns would have to be shut down. In the Soviet economy no such thing has been or is taking place. On the contrary, heavy industry has been and is developing there more rapidly than light industry, regardless of whether current profitability of light industry is higher than that of heavy industry. This is possible, since the proportional distribution of labor among various branches of production is not regulated by the law of value nor by the current profitability of individual concerns and branches of production. Rather, it is regulated by the basic economic laws of Socialism, which gives precedence to production of capital goods (means of production) over consumer goods, so that production may grow uninterruptedly.[39]

However, the financial planning system now takes on elements of the evidence function. Financial control magnitudes logically assume characteristics of directive criteria. Constructing a common measure of all outlays and all receipts necessarily implies weighing individual items and unavoidably passes judgment as to their relative importance. The common measure indicates that, insofar as economic tasks are expressed in financial form and insofar as their fulfillment is controlled by financial criteria materially different, input and output items evaluated with equal financial indexes must be equally valuable representatives of the financial abstraction, "economic performance." In particular, financial stimuli of the fund-and-premium system establish in this sense an abstract relationship between performance and compensation, for the entire enterprise as for individuals, and provide the financial pressure means that are intended to assure adherence to the specified, contractually planned obligations, namely "money penalties, forfeits, fines for injury, resulting from nonfulfillment of the agreement" [40] and a similar abstract relationship for inadequate performance and penalty at least for the enterprise as a whole. Neither of these affects planned performance for specific material, but merely indicates that the financial abstraction of a task is being accomplished, regardless of the material embodiment of this abstraction.

It is conceivable that such a measure is used only to determine the relative valuation of individual increased material performance above plan obligation (exceeding the norm), while planned obligation itself remains untouched in its material composition, so that no material means of production may be neglected nor may any input norm be exceeded. Even with such limited application, the financial measure exercises directing effects. It determines in which direction economic energies are being exerted, insofar as they suffice for increased achievements. If, for example, a certain increased output is overvalued financially, it will attract increased performance energies that would have created greater utility in another direction, in terms of aggregate economic goal-setting.

However, improvement in the partial material performance coefficient (norms) is not the only possible type of economic performance. Economic choice, i.e., the distribution of economic energies among different purposes and selection of most suitable means and methods to realize individual purposes, likewise represents the view of performance. (What is the maximization principle otherwise?) This performance, by shifting or exchanging material input and output items, cannot be distinguished financially from performances in plan fulfillment by exceeding material norms. Both are expressed either in a lowering of the financial input figure of costs or in an increase in the financial achievement figure, in output. To the extent that lower economic units are free to dispose of their output, and as long as control of their economic activity is effective from the financial view only, efforts must be made to improve visible performance also by exercising economic choice, i.e., by substituting cheaper items of input for higher valued ones (assuming constant financial output), and by improving items of output higher valued financially for lower valued ones (assuming constant input).

The tendency to accept financial criteria as lead criteria, in this sense, appears to be illegal and is opposed from above insofar as it pertains to individual areas of economic jurisdiction. "Complaints appear frequently in the Soviet press that enterprises violate their orders regarding assortment and relative proportions of various items in their total output, and yet exceed their production plan in terms of the value of total production." [41] For, "in view of the fact that different products require varying inputs of labor and yield varying profits, many enterprises strive to fulfill the plan primarily by producing the goods which promise to fulfill the prime cost plan." [42] Thus Tureckij reports,

With high profitability (15-25 per cent and more) for individual categories of output of ferrous metallurgy the deficits in many other categories of metal production amounted to 15 to 20 per cent and more in recent years. Examination of plan fulfillment of ferrous metallurgy for 1938 shows that the least percentual fulfillment, in the first instance, pertains to the latter "unprofitable" production categories. The same situation was observed in various branches of nonferrous metallurgy. Nonfulfillment of production plan for ferrous sulphite, and simultaneous overfulfillment of the production plan for copper ore, under the same ore management, is largely explained by the varying relationship between factory prices and planned prime costs of these two categories of production.[43]

This phenomenon is contested most vigorously. It is the focal point of public economic-political discussion and such importance is attached to it that it was made the subject of a resolution of the XVIII Party Conference.[44] Particularly, repeated reference is made to the fact that the plan is not only financial but must be fulfilled in accordance with its material position; "violating plan discipline" is threatened with loss of premium claims won for financial performance and ultimately with further penalties. "Government has requested the ministries and top managers to adhere strictly to existing orders, which forbid premiums for overfulfillment of plan for such products for which there is no need. The plan is to be considered fulfilled only if the requirements as to assortment, type, and quality of output have been observed. The existing premium system for managerial personnel considers fulfilling of plan in accordance with nomenclature assortment and quality as much as with gross output." [45]

However, since the directional effect of financial magnitudes has in essence been applied, such a conflict as indicated must ultimately be unsuccessful. It will have to be decided whether to consider this effect in shaping the financial planning system, to build it into the directed economic system as positive directive means, to use it in planning.

Thus we find an occasional direct appeal to financial self-interest of enterprises, outside the realm of mere execution of plans. Decisions are left to them, which they are to make on the basis of financial criteria.

Consistent use of cheaper materials and equipment, and crediting these savings to the managing personnel of concerns and departments which realized them, lowers production costs of the concern. This procedure stimulates the economic initiative of production concerns and purchasing departments[46] to substitute cheaper for expensive materials. For example, the director of the coke and chemical works of Nizne-Tagil, after *khozraschet* had been introduced in the plant, refused to accept some processed parts made of new metal, until he had used up the supplies of his concern. Practical experience of many concerns shows that under this system, producers are accustomed to substitute cheaper for expensive materials and to make maximum use of waste and by-products.

Khozraschet within the enterprise also stimulates better organization of specialization and cooperation among concerns and enterprises. For example, during the war, the metallurgical combine of Kuzneck used to produce its own tools and chemicals. When *khozraschet* was introduced in the combine, production of these items, which was unprofitable for the equipment of the factory and increased the costs of their main products, was replaced by orders placed with chemical and instrument factories.[47]

However, these lead effects are beginning to be considered in shaping the price system.

> From the point of view of stimulating fulfillment of economic plans by *khozraschet,* not only is profitability of the enterprise as a whole significant, but also the profitability of producing individual types of products in the assortment it produces. The assortment plan is a binding obligation of every enterprise to the State. Financial results are intended to stimulate not only the completion of the production program of the enterprise as a whole, but also its execution as to variety of products. Incorrect determination of profitability of individual types of products of the enterprise may lead to noticeable distortion of assortments.[48]

> Differences in profitability of individual types of products are also established for the purpose of stimulating introduction of new assortments of products, in order to assure plan fulfillment of products of particular economic significance, for example, particularly important forms of rolled metal, etc.[49]

It should be added that the basically negative attitude taken toward evidence function of money and the directive effects of financial magnitudes are not consistently carried out. In the first place, the overemphasis on the significance of accumulation for the development of the economy and the resultant stressing of abstract excess performance, of profit, of profitability as source of accumulation, represents a certain glorification of financial success as such, namely insofar as it is devoted to a specific purpose. As we observed, industrial growth is in no way logically reconcilable with limitation of profitability indicated by its place in the plan. It is significant that the accumulation effort was in general the starting point for the introduction of *khozras-chet*. Thus Stalin gave the following reason for the necessity of *khozraschet,* right after its beginning:

> Prerequisite for every industrialization—which was the avowed objective of the Soviet government—is accumulation. In the development of capitalist countries, foreign credits are available as sources of accumulation. This source is closed to the Soviet Union. The immediately available sources of new accumulation, namely light industry, agriculture, and budgetary surpluses of the State are inadequate. Therefore, what remains? Heavy industry remains. Surpluses must therefore also be realized from heavy industry, and particularly from machine construction. What is necessary to accomplish this? Removal of economic waste, mobilization of internal sources of aid to industry, adoption and consolidation of the profitability principle in all our concerns, systematic lowering of prime costs, increasing accumulation in all branches of industry, without exception.[50]

It is of course possible to interpret the accumulation effort in kind. Expressed better, accumulation is here merely financial conversion of the material process, of increasing productivity more than consumption, so that supplementary economic means are released for capital formation, for "industrial growth." The statement by Stalin, thus interpreted, becomes: no further means can be realized by limiting consumption; if we need further means, we can obtain them only by improving the coefficient of performance. Since this relationship, that increased productivity creates surplus product, benefiting the acceleration of industrial growth, can be formulated clearly in material terms, adherence to financial conversion is all the more astonishing. It shows that the relationship has not been clearly thought through.

This becomes particularly apparent in the thought with the aid of which it is intended to resolve the contradiction that on the one hand there is pronounced emphasis on profitability, while on the other it is rejected as lead criteria. This is likewise traceable to Stalin. It pertains to the distinction between short-term and long-term profitability.

It is maintained that collective—and Soviet—economies are not altogether profitable, that they consume enormous means. . . . it would be more appropriate to dissolve them and to retain only those concerns which are profitable. But only those people who understand nothing of the problems of economics . . . can talk that way. More than half of the textile works were unprofitable a few years ago. Some of our comrades advised us at that time to shut down these plants. Where would we have gotten, if we had followed their advice? . . . We would have destroyed our budding industry in consequence. What did we do then? We waited more than a year and as a result the whole textile industry became profitable. And our auto works in the City Gorki? Or our iron ore industry, which likewise is unprofitable for the time being. Should we perhaps shut it down, comrades? If profitability is interpreted in this manner, we would have to develop only a few branches of industry with all our might, and indeed only those which yielded the largest returns: for example, confectionery wares, milled products, perfumery, knit goods, toy industries, etc. Of course I am not opposed to developing these industrial branches, but in the first place they cannot be developed without machine equipment and fuel, which heavy industry provides for them. Secondly, industrialization cannot be based on them. This is the question, comrades—profitability cannot be viewed commercially, from a short-run point of view. Profitability must be viewed from the standpoint of

the entire economy, in the perspective of several years.[51]
Thus *khozraschet* and the struggle for profitability do not
preclude the construction of enterprises that are unprofitable for the time being. But the problem is to strengthen
khozraschet by lowering costs and increasing the profitability of enterprises.[52]

This reference to the viewpoint of long-term profitability
appears at times immediately beside its complete rejection by the same author. One says, in the same breath as it
were: development of industrial branches does not depend
on profitability at all—and profitability will (must?) appear
in the course of years. Thus it is clear to the economic
thinker that the second argument means complete recognition of profitability as a directive criterion.

Finally it must be pointed out that, in a certain sense,
financial magnitudes are with certain reservations used
obviously and without reflection as directing criteria. For
there can be no doubt that the height of total costs is not
the sole determinant of choice of production method to
attain a given production goal, yet it is given careful consideration in making this decision. Furthermore, it may be
assumed that, in the choice among different projects (production goals), the height of costs has a certain significance.
Because of the rare and always only casual and unsystematic
utterances as to the principles that govern setting up of the
plan, neither can be confirmed with the certainty with which
the remaining facts as to financial planning have been
presented. However, it follows directly from the entire
discussion. In the first place, it should be pointed out that
money calculation, according to official doctrine, is the
temporary representation of a pure labor hour calculation

that is not yet possible because of the unequal valuation of various physical types of labor, and thus actually represents weighing interrelated labor performances.

> But it is also impossible to dispense with money accounting in the State sector. In the Socialist stage there are differences in State enterprises between skilled and unskilled labor, between mental and physical labor. These differences in the types of labor have important economic significance. Skilled labor produces greater value per unit of time than does unskilled labor. This unequal value of labor makes it impossible to compare labor time of one worker with that of another. Consequently, material calculation of socially necessary labor in terms of output or labor time units directly is inadequate. It is therefore necessary to retain money accounting, which combines the differently valued types of social labor into a uniform abstract labor concept.[53]

According to the proclaimed basic principle of increasing labor productivity, lowering this financial expenditure for labor per unit of output must with minor exceptions be the guiding view in directing production.

Furthermore, reference must here be made to the discussion of the question of the effectiveness criterion that has taken place in the Soviet Union in recent years. This is a strange attempt to deal altogether theoretically with principles of plan formation and at the same time to ascribe planning decisions of definitive significance to financial criteria. This is of course the chief reproach made to the adherents to the effectiveness criterion, and to begin with it appears to be telling for the situations there. In this connection it is, however, important, in turn, that authors who reject the effectiveness criterion with such arguments express or assume planning according to minimum costs—although limited by certain general reservations—as an important investment-planning principle. For example, Orlov and Romanov call "prime costs of production" one of the eight most important indexes on the basis of which investment decisions are to be made,[54] and Levine and Mstislavskij provide numerical illustrations for such problems of choice in which the heights of costs, other things being equal, are decisive.[54] Elsewhere also it occurs wherever objections are raised to the point of view of minimizing costs, not because costs as a criterion are to be considered meaningless as such, but only because presumably they cannot reflect particular definite conditions, which should also be considered.

The lack of clarity and the contradictory nature of the attitude toward the evidence function of money, here presented, rests on a misconception of it, as briefly indicated at the outset. The directing effects of money are considered as something absolute but, in relation to guiding planned production, as autonomous; it is not recognized that, with logical development of the financial system, they are merely derived from the preceding fundamental material decisions, that they achieve nothing but the optimal execution of the prescribed basic material concept of the plan (namely the desired material end-purpose assortment as planned), by consistent measurement and by allocation of economic divisible quantities accordingly.

This is particularly so for an understanding of profitability, of gain. It is not seen that, in a consistent value system, profit is not an end in itself, but merely indicates that here the production of certain divisible quantities has not yet experienced the required optimal measurement in the interest of the comprehensively set goal, and shows the agency directing the requisite energies and means toward the production of inadequately treated divisible quantities.

It is not realized that no production necessary for the set final purpose can be unprofitable, since this necessity must find expression in the value, in an appropriate setting of price. Instead, it is believed that here the abstract goal displaces the concrete one, that production oriented to profitability may by the quest for profit be derived from material fulfillment of purpose. Aside from a certain bias in individualistic economic thinking, there are perhaps two general trends of thought that are relevant. On the one hand, concepts from the area of the Marxist system are significant: on the other hand, of capitalistic enterprise, stumbling from one crisis to another in its quest for profits, and thus missing the ultimate purpose of the economy, production of consumption values. "Goal of Capitalistic production is the creation and enlargement of surplus value, the sweating out of profits. To attain this goal, enormous productive powers are destroyed. In contrast herewith, the goal of Socialist production consists of assuring maximum satisfaction of man's material and cultural needs." [56] Or ". . . under Capitalism there is a contradiction between the concept of pecuniary profitability or the remunerativeness of the individual enterprise and the rational use of productive powers." [57] On the other hand, it is believed that relating production to profit will favor the consumers at the expense of capital formation, of "industrial development." Underlying this is experience, fallaciously generalized, of the restoration years. Actually, in a correctly coordinated planning system, planning need not give consumers more than it pleases, aside from the unavoidable relation between willingness to produce and share in consumption, even if the planning system uses financial methods of guidance. But in the restoration years there was an error of coordination in this respect. The financial consumption component was kept larger than the material one. This was perhaps partly because of inadequate command of the planning apparatus, and also because use was made of the popular illusion of nominal income, prevailing in all countries in times of particular strain, to increase the willingness of the people to work, more than could be expected at the given level of consumption. The excess purchasing power thus created had to find expression in a corresponding distorted profitability relationship in favor of the goods desired with this excess purchasing power.[58] Or, on the other hand and for similar reasons, shortsighted financial policy kept too low the prices of heavy industry, which ranked highest in the material purpose scale.[59] With such disturbance of financial relationships and distortion of financial proportions, financial criteria obviously could not exercise an equitable, systematic guidance effect. Moreover, here also the mixture of questions of formal consistency of the price system, likewise widespread among us in the West, and the origin of ultimate production goals (controversy as to "consumer sovereignty") will certainly exercise its influence.

The same basic error will also occur if profit is accepted as partial economic goal. It is not sought positively, merely as a derivative criterion of fundamental economic purpose, but as absolute, as financial return in itself. Its meaning is seen, insofar as it promotes accumulation and hence industrial development. This concept arises likewise, paradoxically, from the same Marxist source as the rejection of profit as a guiding criterion. Marx teaches that surplus value, profit, is the source of accumulation, and thus Socialist surplus value is desired to promote accumulation. Moreover, viewed superficially, profit is also the source of accumulation in Soviet reality, particularly if the turnover tax is included, which is designated part of Socialist surplus value as anticipated profit. The mistake that is made here is the inadmissible combination of two questions: (1) as to the source of investment means, which is at the same time a question of the distribution of the given Gross National Product (between consumption and saving) and (2) as to the choice of investment of given means which, with given division of output (i.e., with end purposes of production, including division of economic efforts between present and future services), are designed to realize the technically possible optimum output. Profit has essential significance only in the second problem area (No. 2 above). It is not important because of its size, but only as an indication that here the application of means has not been extended remuneratively to the margin. Accumulation, on the other hand, is a question of drawing off produced income for capital formation, in the Soviet case almost exclusively by means of taxation, and thus falls into the first problem area. The relations of profit to it are purely accidental; neither does profit have to serve accumulation nor is accumulation dependent on profit.

Insofar as individual prices and costs are accepted as directive magnitudes, it is not clear whether they can perform this function meaningfully merely in a consistently developed price system. This becomes particularly apparent where it is intended to ascribe a limited subsidiary significance to cost and price indexes as directive criteria in making economic decisions, namely, after "economic need," "over-all economic combinations," the necessity for maintaining over-all economic proportions, the specific scarcity of rare materials, and the like, are considered. Thus this assumes that the price system does not consider all these factors. However, every value and price system is meaningful only insofar as it comprehends the aggregate of economic purposes in their relative significance, and all the conditions needed to realize these purposes. It is actually only a method of grasping this over-all relationship and of making its consistency apparent. The exclusion of particular conditions thus takes away the evidence value from the entire system. If financial magnitudes are not given total directive effect, it is a mistake to consider them at all.

The Soviet planning system has thus far not succeeded in constructing this logical financial aggregative relationship, in which financial proportions correspond with set production goals. Since, however, as shown in this section, the introduction of money as an economic guiding instrument could not be avoided, the financial guidance system presents the picture of casuistic experimentation, in order to correct observed mistakes in individual cases and to attain necessary effects without, however, attaining a meaningful aggregate financial coordination, and without an actual equilibrium of items equally valued financially. In this connection, particular significance attaches to the tensions between the system of financial guidance and the continued existence of material planning. The relationship of these two methods of guidance to each other will next be investigated.

3

Relationship Between Material and Financial Guidance and Division of Economic Decision-Making Authority

Distinguishing Characteristics of the Material Method of Guidance

IN THE preceding chapter we saw that material control of the activity of lower agencies of economic administration is inadequate, and that this leads to the introduction of money accounting and the development of a financial system of guidance. But this system of financial guidance, as was shown further, allowed some choice and decision-making to the lower agencies. We must now examine how this financial guidance system is related to the material system of guidance with which our exposition began, and in particular the manner in which the position of the lower

agencies in the material guidance system is reconciled with
that assigned to them by the financial guidance system.

To begin with, the meaning of material guidance of production, in contrast with financial guidance, must be clari-
fied. Only a few references to this question are found in the
available source materials, since the question could not even
be asked in this form in the Soviet Union because of the
lack of theoretical premises. It thus becomes necessary to
introduce a few basic theoretical considerations here.

Usually the two concepts, material and financial guidance
of production, are assumed to correspond to centralized and
decentralized guidance, respectively. Financial production
guidance means that a substantial number of immediate
production guiding agencies undertake the determination
of their particular material production program independently, and that in so doing they are guided by financial
criteria. Material production guidance, on the other hand,
is intended to mean that the many agencies guiding production directly have their material production program
prescribed from above by the "central authority." [1] Insofar
as planned economy, i.e., "centrally administered economy"
is understood as "material production guidance," the concept implies that virtually the entire economy, with few exceptions, is guided by a single will, that it is "one head" that
makes all decisions, and, in principle, determines the course
of all subordinate processes. "This 'centrally directed' economic system is distinguished by the fact that guiding the
daily economic activity of a community proceeds on the
basis of the plans of a central office." [2]

The same idea of the supremacy of one will, that of the
Party as representative of the working class, i.e., the entire
working population, is also found throughout the plan in
the Soviet Union. "The policy of the Party and of the State

appears as a force directing and organizing the development of the economy in planned order, on the basis of known laws of Socialism. . . . Socialist planning is subordinated to realizing economic-political aims, set for the country by the Party and the Soviet State." [3]

In seeking the limitations of this centralization, the discussion does not center primarily around the limits growing out of the logic of the situation but relates to the way in which authority is intentionally relaxed by granting powers that might be exercised by the central office to other members of the economic body. Throughout, the position of all consumers and workers is considered. The relaxation thus relates to the greater or lesser influence left to them as to the composition of their share in consumption on the one hand and the choice of their place of employment on the other.[4] It is, therefore, not a matter of the degree of centralization within the administration making actual production decisions, but rather the determination of the goals to which the procedure is ultimately subordinated.

Naturally production decisions cannot be made by "one head" in the literal sense. Rather, it requires a whole administrative apparatus, since the size of the population, land area, and production activity make it impossible for a single leading person to supervise continuously all economic processes, to give detailed directions, and to see that they are carried out. However, the insertion of the administrative apparatus is viewed primarily as an organizational-technical measure that is not to alter anything in the rule of one will in the entire economy; the activity of this apparatus is understood as mere implementation of the central will. "Hence an administrative apparatus with numerous officials exists, which—in a completely centrally administered economy—

alone* undertakes to draw up economic plans, gives detailed instructions to existing concerns as to what they are to produce, carries out allocation of raw materials and intermediate products among individual concerns, orders reconstruction or alteration of existing plans, assigns places of employment to the labor force, distributes consumer goods among individuals, and controls the carrying out of all directives." [5] This is expressed with particular clarity by Hensel.[6] He describes the central planning system as "guiding apparatus," "encompassing the organization of the entire national economy," and arranged into ministries, chief divisions, and specialized divisions. Then he says, "in what follows we will proceed with the assumption that a complete, rationally constructed and functioning guiding organization exists, which represents a complete instrument of the central administration. Within it no will is considered unless it is the will of the central administration, or conforms with it." As practical limitations on the acceptance of this central will only the following are named at this point: Duplicate organizations and other useless forms of the organizational structure, resulting in inadequate coordination of the guiding measures, particularly in contradictory orders to individual concerns and wrong instructions of all kinds. Where such defects are avoided, the activities of the lower directing agencies would have to be determined by nothing but the strict execution of the will of the central authority, and therefore be synonymous with this will.

Since there are actually various heads that jointly make the individual decisions constituting the central plan and central will, the dangers of "branch monopolistic viewpoints" among the leaders of separate specialized divisions

* Italics supplied by editor of translation.

become apparent, with resultant "anarchistic group conflict." Thus the question is raised whether it will be possible
to obtain the interest and willingness of cooperating heads
to carry out the central plan.[7] This question, however,
assumes that such action is required, and thus is possible
with proper behavior of the participants.

The objection raised primarily by Eucken[8] goes farthest
in asserting that the centrally administered economy is incapable of integrating the partial plans of all these administrative agencies in formulating the central plan, so that the
degree of realization of individually set objectives is arranged according to their importance, and the means for
their realization are distributed and combined with a view
to maximizing fulfillment of purpose. For this implies that
actually a majority of heads and agencies makes planning
decisions, and that the decisions of this multiplicity need
coordination. Eucken is undoubtedly correct in asserting
that the diversity of the posed problem vastly exceeds the
powers of comprehension and of integration by a single head,
and that therefore a consistent coordination of all decisions
of choice, with a view to maximizing fulfillment of purpose,
is impossible without monetary accounting and consistent
price formation.[9] But he presents the argument solely for
this purpose, and pays no further attention to the phenomenon of the number of participants in planning and the
principles that then govern the division of their activity or
the delimiting of their decision-making authority. Thus his
argument may justly be viewed as merely an assertion that
central planning is incapable of a purposive coordination of
all partial processes in accordance with the maximization
principle, but that nevertheless, accidentally, it undertakes
a somewhat systematic coordination, which finally means
central determining of all partial processes.[10]

This consideration of the material planning system as a "centrally" directed one undoubtedly expresses a justifiable point of view. However, its onesidedness obstructs insight into the essential characteristics that distinguish a material planning and guiding system from a purely financial one. Contrasting these two systems of guiding as *centralized** and *decentralized,** moreover, expresses the contrast somewhat too pointedly. The economic process possesses the same complexity, whether guided financially or materially. Hence, the number of agencies making direct specific production decisions must also be approximately the same,[11] since the area within which one head with human power of perception (imaginative power) and coordinating ability can make specific decisions is independent of the system of guidance. Moreover, it cannot be a question as to whether these lower agencies, guiding production directly, are merely tied to material planning or are relatively free (with "decentralized" self-directed planning). It is a major aim of market economy theory to show that the formal, independent agencies, the free owners and enterprisers, are bound by self-interest, stimulated by threat of loss of livelihood, into a higher usefulness lying beyond their sphere of interests and, as a rule, even beyond their horizon. But this tie results from abstract rules and criteria. This indirect, formal tie is to be contrasted with a specific, proximate tie of the material, planned economy, resulting from direct regulation.

The contrast between tying to formal, general behavior norms and tying to specific directives does not tell as much as one would suspect at first sight. There is no doubt that the concrete directives coming from the highest coordinating authority cannot completely determine the activities of the lower agencies. The directives of this authority, if they are

* Italics supplied by editor of translation.

to be all-embracing, must in some way be general. The problem thus remains for the lower agencies to convert these general directives into specific actions, and in so doing, room is left for them to make their own decision.

Next, it is necessary to examine in what sense a material directive may be "general," and what the relation is between this general directive of the higher authorities and the actual measures of the lowest agencies. We may distinguish two types of generalization: (1) those that are aggregative (or global); and (2) those that are *schematic.** In an aggregative (lump-sum) generalization, numerous individual components are combined into an aggregate amount in order to establish a common perimeter that delimits their area of activity and claims, and the area of tasks, without determining their interrelationship or differentiation within the delimited area. It differs from the financial tie as follows: the financial tie permits every agency to exchange units of use and means over the entire area, without limitation; there is therefore no hierarchical arrangement of agencies. All production-guiding agencies are rather on the same level, and connected directly by the financial medium into exchange relationships. For this the exchange relations of end products and means are established. Material combination in the form of aggregatives or global planning, on the other hand, restrict the area, from step to step, within a hierarchically arranged system of production-guiding agencies, in which the agencies may undertake exchange of end products and means. Exchange outside this area is possible only by way of the higher authorities. But exchange relations in this delimited area are left to the judgment of the directly deciding agencies.

Global planning takes place particularly where quantities

* Italics supplied by editor of translation.

are involved, with sharp differentiation between their origin and determination of their use. It is therefore significant for economic guidance, since it involves production and distribution of an extensively complex assortment of goods. Decisions as to quantities made by the highest central authority can relate only to general supply categories and commodity groups that incorporate a multiplicity of requirements and goods of varied local, personal, and material significance.[12] Thus, for example, a produced quantity of, say, 100,000 tons of steel tells us nothing; it must first be determined whether cast steel, rolled steel of this or that quality, special steel, steel for rails, tractors, lathes, roofing-plates, or steel for tractors for this or that district, etc., is intended. Such detailed designation puts meaning into the proposed quantity of 100,000 tons of steel. This particularization is continued to the lowest agencies, giving direct orders for the production of individual quantities. The lump-sum quantities with which the central authority works thus obtain their meaning from the particular support provided by these lower agencies; they originate only as a result of assembling these bases, and only in this manner do they become meaningful.

Schematization (*Schematisierung*) involves reducing the multiplicity of individual processes by uniting or treating alike related similar yet differentiated items.* This facilitates the over-all view of many individual components for the higher authorities; the separate components become more apparent to them. Above all, this procedure limits the area in which the lower agencies have decision-making authority while obligating them to make allocations within this area. The function of this particular division of authority to make decisions was to better allocate or dif-

* Translator's Note: Presumably in some form or other of indexes.

ferentiate the lump-sum indicated quotas in order to adapt them to the particular conditions anticipated by the lower agencies only in this particular field. Schematization means on the one hand abandoning differentiation within the aggregates of items, according to their changing composition; on the other, it means regulation without knowledge of the particular circumstances of these separate areas. In both cases it means less efficiency, less fulfillment of purpose, because of their being less suitable measures. The reason why this price is paid, why the useful initiative of the lower agencies is excluded, is either mistrust of the lower units, i.e., suspicion that they will not exercise their authority in the public interest or in the interest of the central agency but out of ignorance of fact, or it is the recognition of the incompetence of these agencies, lacking adequate intellectual independence and judgment, to make objective decisions. Schematization, in this sense, actually means definite tying of lower agencies to the decisions of higher authorities, without allowing an area to show individual competence. This is truly centralization. But complete centralization cannot be built on this method of centralization. Schematic directives also contain specific and extensive determination of individual action components. Because of the complexity that cannot be encompassed in any one model, they cannot be too far removed from the centralized directives, for otherwise they would lose their applicability and hence their determinative effectiveness. Thus the large gap between central authority and lower units cannot be completely bridged by schematization. To be sure, it reduces the number of agencies having individual decision-making power. However, it does not alter the fact that even a so-called centrally administered economy shows a number of lower agencies with independent decision-making power

and creative possibilities. Hence the *more important** relationship between higher and lower agencies remains that
of lump-sum planning (*Pauschalizierung*) and specific direction of the use of resources (*Konkretisierung*).

The central authority alone, as we see, is unable to produce a closed system of planned tasks; it is dependent on the
cooperation of the lower agencies. These actually establish
the relationship of individual tasks to reality and from this
provide the items from which are assembled the global
values with which the central authority works. This operation of lower units is independent in the area delineated by
the central or next higher authority. While thus the material guidance system is not a "completely centralized"
one, conversely, the financial guidance system can by no
means dispense with it. In modern, predominantly *market-
oriented economies** there is a central authority that endeavors to shape the aggregate economic process by managing currency, administering taxes, and by collective state
economic activity, by restrictive economic legislation, and
even by more far-reaching intervention. *Competitive socialistic** concepts show that the central authority may be entrusted with even more completely all-embracing tasks in a
purely financial guidance system.

But it would seem that the functions of the central agency
are more highly developed in a materially directed
economy. This becomes apparent in the hierarchical structure of the directing apparatus emanating from the center.
However, such a general observation is inadequate because
the task still remains to determine the *particular functions**
of this hierarchically constructed guidance apparatus.

One might be inclined to see this particular feature in
the decisions of the agency that sets the *ultimate economic*

* Italics supplied by editor of translation.

*goals** to be realized. The material method of guidance thus would be distinguished from the financial method, in that in the former the central authority decides the ultimate goal to be realized, while, if financial guidance prevails, the goal decision is left to consumers. This presentation plays an important role in scientific discussion of planned economy versus market economy. In this discussion authors investigate variously, and not always unambiguously, the relationship between the material method and the financial method of guidance. Eucken, for example, distinguishes sharply between the centrally administered and the market economy[13] in the latest edition of his *Principles*. Here he asserts that, if the leadership of a centrally managed economy "sought to use demand as an index of needs of the population," it would be "endeavoring to draw up its economic plan by considering the economic plans of the citizens of the State," and so "its economic plan would be dependent on the many economic plans of the prospective buyers," and thus "the limits of the centrally directed economy would be reached or exceeded" so that this case could be "classified as an exchange economy." [14] In Hensel, the criteria that distinguish his models of "completely centralized" from "complete decentralization of the economic process" [15] include the determination of the *final goal** by the political central authority in one case, by consumers in the other.[16]

Actually, it is impossible to draw such a distinction. In the first place, such a distinction inadmissively has limited "demand" to purely private demand, at least for the market economy, whereas among the ultimate purposes served by every economy there are the collective needs and material requirements of the state. The state ultimately decides upon

* Italics supplied by editor of translation.

the satisfaction of these community needs,[17] regardless of whether it obtains the requisite means therefore by direct appropriation or withdraws them first by the roundabout method of taxation from the resources of the private sector; whether it carries out the requisite production tasks entirely on its own or with participation of private enterprise in filling state orders; whether the measurement of the extent of fulfilling the purpose is immediately expressed in material form or derived from a sum of money made available for this purpose. The political, central authority, however, appearing here as "large-scale placer of orders," is not a market participant beside others, but in its hand rests the responsible shaping of the aggregate economic process; thus economically it is throughout a complete central agency. Such a central agency decides the choice of goal for a substantial portion of economic goals, *regardless of guidance system and method of guidance.** Hence the characteristic of the agency, making decisions as to ultimate goal, is unsuited as sign of the peculiarity of the material guidance method.

Moreover, a rigorous distinction cannot be drawn even in the choice of objectives relative to *private** demand. In the first place, the central authority must necessarily, regardless of system and method of guidance, limit aggregate private demand relative to communal needs. This problem necessarily follows from the other, i.e., limiting various communal needs relative to available means. It involves a certain weighing and judging of individual items of private demand, for without weighing the specific meaning of the significance of the relationship between separate public and private requirements, the requisite limitation of communal needs cannot be achieved. This can be done only

* Italics supplied by editor of translation.

from the over-all point of view of the community, the state.[18]

How far the state also wants to postulate the positive composition of private consumption on this limiting evaluation is basically a political decision. Around the pros and cons thereof revolve an essential part of the discussion of the merits of a planned economy, and various possible behavior patterns in graduated models have been developed.[19] For both basic patterns of behavior increasingly serious views are expressed. The influencing of private consumption is from the point of communal interest in itself the consequence of state responsibility for public welfare, and scarcely any state will want to divest itself of this responsibility.[20] On the other hand, such public interest in shaping private consumption exists only in certain connections, and even there the central authority must recognize that, in some respects, the individual consumer is better able to judge what is good for him, also from the view of public interest, than the central agency with its crude methods of evaluation by its extensive bureaucratic managerial apparatus, created for this purpose. Beyond that, there might be a common interest in allowing the individual citizen some free choice also in his private life, even if this freedom were abused, since in expressing his wishes he becomes ultimately the bearer of communal wishes and interests. From this limited right of both basic types of behavior, meaningless as applied rigorously to one type, arises the necessity of a compromise, a freedom of consumer choice, restricted by the state. Such a compromise is sought in almost all known systems of guidance, regardless of the method of guidance employed.

Thus there is no rigorous coupling (*Koppelung*) of centralized shaping of private consumption and material guidance, and freedom of choice by consumers and financial guidance. Rather the state can influence the composition of private consumption extensively also with financial means; on the other hand, the application of the material method of planning must not exclude every means of influencing consumers in shaping their consumption. As extreme cases, we may imagine either of the following situations: (1) a financial system of guidance whose ultimate values rest entirely on state valuations. This, to be sure, would have to be protected against the influences of sums of money in the hands of consumers, which they might employ otherwise by supplemental control or by introducing another system of distribution; (2) a material guidance system subordinated to the established will of the consumers, as statistically determined, or aided solely by consumers' money not entering into the production sphere.[21] But this indicates again that dividing decision as to the ultimate goals to be realized does not distinguish the material method of guidance from the financial method.

If the distinguishing feature of the material method of guidance does not lie in the determination of goal, it must be sought in the procedure used to guide production in accordance with the given directives. It is here a question of choice of combinations of means of production, of measurement of input of various types of production means for individual production goals, and of arranging the means in graduated sequence, insofar as they are not original factors of production but intermediate products. The allocation of separate material input items for individual production goals must always be carried out by an extensive apparatus of individual directing agencies, in accordance with the multiplicity of goals as well as of possible production combinations. However, these decisions must be made to harmonize, for individual production processes must supplement each other so that for all quantities produced the requisite input items are available, and so that all available production means and factors find use in production.

Two possibilities exist for establishing this equilibrium. One is the "market" equilibrium. Its mechanism is familiar. Influenced by the significance of a good for the production of other goods or ultimately for the fulfillment of purpose, the height of its price regulates the extent of its employment ("demand") relative to its production costs, i.e., to the alternative use possibilities of its expendable elements and the extent of its production ("supply"). Thus stimuli to change in quantity occur in the production and use of every good until equilibrium results.

The relationship among separate equilibrating measures that must all be interrelated because the complementarity of all intermediate stages in every separate production process must be preserved—this relationship depends on the fact that from the outset every individual guiding unit will undertake only such changes in its allocations as will preserve this complementarity. It is able to do this, since in its allocations no restrictions are placed in any area as to the interchangeability of units of ends and means. It is bound only by its responsibility (i.e., its direct interest) to see that, under its guidance, production processes are successful.

Since the equilibrating processes for every separate good are regulated by money prices as representatives of possible exchange relationships of the goods, and the separate directing agencies have to harmonize the significance of the goods in their realm of responsibility with these money prices, the financial valuation system is necessarily established, which is indispensable for shaping production from optimum views. This equilibrating method may be designated the "financially guided" method.

In the other way of bringing about equilibrium, the separate output and input items of a good are equated directly, and equilibrium is brought about by increasing output and decreasing consumption. We may therefore call this the method of equilibrating by material-balancing.

The characteristic of this method lies in the fact that equilibrating of a good is not brought about by the manifold actions of individual guiding agencies (producers) but by the decisions of a balancing central agency. In consequence, individual agencies also lose their ability to preserve the relationship between separate input and output items within the area of their responsibility; rather, the complementarity of all equilibrating measures must be assured by the balancing central agency. It must therefore establish the aggregate relationships among all separate equilibrating areas that are as such connected individually.

But, as previously shown, this cannot be rigorously carried out. The ultimate fact created by the problem of coordination is the *complexity** of this relationship, which cannot be supervised by a *single** agency. That is why it is necessary to assemble the individual items into lump-sum magnitudes in order to make supervision possible. This is particularly true of separate input and output items. In place of plows, sewing machines, mowing machines, etc., of particular types, the expression "agricultural machines" appears; all sorts of fabrics are combined, among others, as "dress materials," "clothing materials," "wash materials," "hosiery," etc. In like aggregative manner the relationship between individual material input and output types must

* Italics supplied by editor of translation.

be expressed, for only with knowledge of these relationships is it possible to measure effects of changes in items of one commodity balance as compared with other commodity balances. The lump-sum norms described in "Participation of Central and Lower Agencies in Drawing Up of the Plan," Chapter 1, serve this purpose. For example, they give an idea as to how much leather, metal, labor power, plant capacity, and the like, on an average, are required for 1,000 pairs of shoes; or how much steel, cement, building material, labor power, and mechanized building equipment is necessary, on an average, for industrial or housing construction having 1,000 cubic meters of built-up space. On the basis of these lump-sum norms it is then possible to determine, in case of disequilibria, the extent of the required reapportionment. For example, it would show, in case of a deficit in the building material balance, by how much housing construction would have to be reduced if it were intended to correct the deficit at its expense and what quantities of other materials and workers would be released in consequence.[22]

This illustration shows that the composition of groups of commodities must be based upon the degree of substitutability of the items, i.e., their production relationship. For example, it would be nonsense to use steel saved in housing construction to cover a shortage in tractor construction if the type of steel saved could not be so used, or if at least the particular production plans and means were not suited to produce both types of steel. In addition to specialized plants, such a question is also significant as to skilled labor power.

If certain transition periods and conversion outlays are taken into account in addition to ultimate sacrifice of certain qualities, substitutability of the items in some areas is extensive. On the other hand, it might frequently be inadequate to permit such an extensive assembling of all material planning elements as would really make possible supervision by the highest authority. Thus one is confronted with the choice of either (1) exceeding that which is meaningful in assembling, (2) assuming that the lower units will find a way for conversion, or (3) permitting the equilibrating apparatus of the highest authority to remain as comprehensive in jurisdiction as is necessary to observe all possibilities of integration and to undertake unavoidable incomplete equilibrating. Actually, a compromise among these alternative solutions will always be sought. There will be an apparatus at the highest agency, staffed by many persons, and an executive committee will endeavor to carry out its decisions without having available a further reduced closed system.

The global or lump-sum decisions of the central agency will naturally then have to be made specific and be differentiated. Every decrease or increase in a global item must be distributed among the relevant individual items contained in it. In so doing, all combinations established by the higher authority—the allocation of means for definite tasks—must be coordinated in detail, and only then will it become apparent whether the substitutability assumed by the central authority actually exists, and what reduction in results, owing to costs and loss of time because of the alteration, in reality are connected with it. This performance is therefore the test of the practicability of the equalizing measures taken by the central agency. The possibility of this recourse to the detailed calculations of the lower units also justifies extending assembling beyond the limit set by the condition of interchangeability of the assembled goods.

In view of the multiplicity of goods and relationships,

the assembling process will have to take place in stages. Thus a hierarchically organized system of directing agencies is developed for material balance, even as indicated above for material guidance. Consequently, to be sure, the decisive equilibrating measures are taken at the highest stage of the system; but within the area, delimited by it, the equalizing problem is given anew to the lower agencies at every level. Each subordinate agency in its circumscribed material area has lump-sum delimited production tasks to fulfill, and lump-sum specific quotas of means of production that must suffice. The relationship between decisions made by the higher and lower agencies is that indicated above, i.e., a "lump-sum" or (global) model.

In this connection the "schematic" generalization method described above is significant. By unification of tasks in their specific appearance and by measuring the input of means for their fulfillment, i.e., the methods of production, the entire process is made more intelligible for the higher agencies and independent of calculations of lower agencies; it gives them a more immediate and clearer idea of the effects of prospective equalizing measures. The limits and disadvantages of this method, which in consequence has only supplemental significance, were indicated above.

At all events, we see that in this case a financial valuation system is not developed automatically. The technical unavoidability of its development with financially guided equilibration requires that financial magnitudes be made the vehicle for bringing about balance. The method operates only by way of financial interest in success of the producing units. But then it also guarantees the "correctness" of the value equivalence. Until the value ascribed to a good corresponds with its significance in all the processes in which it participates, an equilibrium will not be achieved, for stimuli to change the supplied or demanded quantities continue to be present. This may therefore be called the indirect method of equilibrating.

In applying the material method, on the other hand, balance is dictated from above by direct material intervention. At all events, the necessity for developing financial magnitudes does not exist, since a condition of equilibrium is attained without it. This also indicates that the tendencies to produce optimal proportions by employing varying quantities of means, which logically derive from application of the financial method, need not pertain under the material method. The question that remains to be answered is whether the creation of a financial valuation system which, as was shown at the beginning of the preceding chapter, is indispensable for the economy to attain an optimum situation, can be combined with the application of the material method of balance.

Relationship Between Determining Goal and Guiding Method

To begin with, the material guiding system will be examined more closely by investigating the relationships that exist between determination of the goal and the method of guidance. As previously indicated, no necessary relationship exists here, yet there are certain similarities and affinities whose elucidation is required for an understanding of the guidance systems.

It must first be recognized that consumer determination of goal requires restricting the area of influence by individuals. This, however, must proceed in such a general form that, within this restricted area of influence, material decisions have not been made in advance, but specific material goals set by individuals may be interchanged optionally at established exchange relationships. This can be accomplished solely by a financial valuation system. Goal-setting by consumers means introducing a type of valuation system, at least in the marketing sector. Now it might be possible, as just indicated, to limit the effectiveness of this valuation system to the marketing sector, if the marketing establishments continued material planning based on demand expressed in material units. But it follows naturally that such a valuation system would also be carried out in the production sector.

The investigation may be carried still further, into the relation between determination of goal and the guiding of use of means needed to attain selected goals: this latter concept includes as an important item establishment of equilibrium between output and consumption. The trend of thought pursued thus far is based entirely on the distinction between setting the goal and determining the use of means, and this distinction is also justified, for ultimately the agency called on to make a decision and the nature of the decision are different. But we must realize that *both types** of decisions are constantly concurrent in the actual guidance process. Viewed as the problem of creating equilibrium we may say: equilibrium can be attained either (1) by substituting available and relatively abundant means for relatively scarce means to fulfill a given task, or (2) by abandoning such goals as must be attained by using particularly scarce means of production in favor of others that will utilize more plentiful means to attain alternative goals, i.e., substituting goals.[23] Thus, every partial disequilibrium may be removed by changing either the goal or the combination of means. In financial guidance, for example, every

* Italics supplied by editor of translation.

disequilibrium affects the market for means of production by raising the price of the scarce means; substituting other production means for it and (insofar as means or goods of first order are needed for attainment), substituting other goals for those originally sought are also made more expensive in consequence. On the other hand, in case of cheapening of a means of production not fully exploited the opposite naturally would take place, i.e., substituting these means and the resultant attained goals for the other means and goals. Similarly also with material guidance, it will be determined in the course of the coordinating process which means are best suited for replacing others, and also which goals can be attained at the expense of others (i.e., how the alternatives for the choice of goals are determined). The choice of goal is ultimately decided on the basis of costs, which are derived concurrently from chosen substitution of means.

In consumer-determined goals the question now arises as to how equilibrating measures in the production process are connected with consumer decisions. This question is particularly important for those production means whose use is far removed from actual production of consumers' goods. Even in financial guidance this relationship is very remote, and depends primarily on the anticipations of individual enterprisers of whom it certainly cannot be said that they are guided by the actual wishes of consumers. However, the connection with the wishes of consumers is considerably stronger here than with material guidance. In material guidance, decisions as to fundamental equilibrating measures, which are likewise decisions as to fundamental proportions of attainment of goal, are made at the level of the *highest guiding agencies.** No matter how much they may

* Italics supplied by editor of translation.

try to guess directly what the wishes of consumers are, or may try to make the data on consumer reactions received from subordinate agencies the basis of their decisions, it remains true that decisions by the higher agencies are much more generalized; they proceed on the basis of *universal conceptions of goals** and consequently are technically much further removed from the specific goals reposing in consumers than the more individualized conceptions of goals of individual enterprisers. All goods are included in this extreme generalization, while with financial guidance a substantial part of production can actually be guided by market reactions of consumers, and so is closely tied to their wishes. Finally, the attachment of individual enterprisers to financial guidance is vital, since financial success of their activity and hence their economic existence, are dependent on the correctness of their anticipations. The attachment of the central guiding agencies, on the other hand, depends on their *good will.**

While, therefore, combining of substitution of goal and substitution of means in the practical guiding process involves a certain detachment from the actual wishes of consumers, such detachment is much more pronounced in material guidance. In addition, the decisions under material guidance are concentrated to a greater degree in a central agency.[24] In general, it may be asserted, financial guidance with setting of goal by the individual consumer represents the more suitable system. But, as has been said, this does not exclude material methods of guidance. It is possible and meaningful that material methods of guidance, in addition to financial methods, are retained by distributing agencies. Hence there is *conceptually** no exclusive connection be-

* Italics supplied by editor of translation.

tween freedom of choice of consumers and the use of financial guidance methods.

Conversely, there is a special connection between determination of goal by the central authority and the financial guidance methods. To explain this we must first consider the manner in which basic financial values are established. We revert once more to the pure financially guided economy, with complete consumer freedom of choice. Here the individual consumer does not make his choice by first valuing separately the individual goals and purposes as well as their unit quantities, by estimating their significance in terms of a common medium (i.e., by making "his intensive value estimate extensive") and arranging them in order of rank, according to his valuation index. Rather his decision proceeds from an immediate material comparison of these goals and purposes, where only *two or three** purposes are considered simultaneously and only a *more or less important** one is determined, and the aggregate order of rank is derived from a succession of such individual decisions. The attempt to fix his entire valuation system numerically in advance must fail. Such established value indexes would again be upset by the valuer when comparing items one with another (in pairs) materially.[25] Man is not a calculating machine, registering his needs or ideas of requirements as fixed quantities. Judgement as to relative importance must be constantly expressed anew, and must be expressed on the basis of one specific concept of purpose (or the meaningful realization of need), measured in terms of another specific concept.

We must now examine the manner in which material order in rank of purposes and goods, resulting from con-

* Italics supplied by editor of translation.

sumers' choosing, is converted into the financial valuation system, i.e., into the prices guiding production. Above all, we must inquire what such conversion means, and to what degree the financial valuation system expressed in terms of prices indicates consumer preference, according to his judgment of the order in rank of purposes and goods. The relationship between these two valuation systems is affected by the fact that the order in rank of goods shifts with changes in their exchange relation, established in the prices. Hence the longer one purpose or aim is postponed, the greater the postponement of another fulfillment of purpose that it requires. Conversely it follows that the higher the price of a good, the greater must be the importance ascribed to it, since it is nevertheless being considered by buyers. Thus price appears as the quantitative expression of the importance attributed to a good.

The objections that may be raised to this conclusion may tentatively be stated as follows: The similarity does not go so far that one could say that a good whose price is three times as high as that of another good is three times as important. What is the assertion "three times as important" intended to say, if the significance of every unit of a good is different? The importance of the next to last demanded unit of a low-valued good may perhaps be greater than that of the next to last unit of a high-valued good, although that of the next unit of the low-valued good may be only minimal.

A threefold consideration is involved in this objection. In the first place, there are no such quantitatively fixed relations in the material order of rank established by the consumer according to purposes and to goods as are shown in the price system. An order of rank recognizes only an "important" or "less important" one.

Secondly, and this is the essence of the objection: prices, at best, indicate the importance of the marginal unit (the "marginal utility") of a good. The order of rank pertains essentially to the intramarginal area; the marginal range represents only a sector of the aggregate aims valued by the consumers. This observation is common knowledge in our economic theory; the so-called second Gossen law says nothing else. However, it is consistent with the possibility of guiding the economy solely with the aid of prices, in terms of production goals set by the state, although this usually is not the case. That is why this point is given particular emphasis here.

In the third place, the height of prices need not even be characteristic of the order of rank in the marginal sector. To show this, I should like to refer to price elasticities of the goods. Elasticity is very low for a series of important goods. That means that the position of these goods in the order of rank of demand is largely independent of their price. In the extreme case of a completely inelastic demand, a specific quantity will be purchased regardless of price, and beyond that none will be purchased. Here it can be seen clearly that the height of the price is not determined by the marginal importance of the good. The importance of the last desired unit may be very high, presumably far higher than the price, while the importance of the first not wanted unit may actually be zero. The nearer determination of price in this case comes from the side of supply, that is, in general, from marginal costs. In the case of goods with inelastic demand the height of the price does not depend primarily on the gradations of the importance attached to successive units by the consumer, but on differences in costs.

This inelasticity of demand has decided practical significance. Decisions of choice made by consumers are not determined by price as extensively as is widely assumed.[26] Hence the marginal sector, in which only the relationship between order of rank of goods and height of prices can exist, loses much of its significance, and shrinks into a mere line of demarcation between goods presumably desired and goods presumably not desired. In such cases, the price of goods has no closer relationship to the conceptual significances attached to it by users.

This does not in the least impair the importance of prices as leading criteria for guiding production. The internal order of rank of the total demanded quantities of respective goods, i.e., their varying significance for the consumer, is unimportant for production. It suffices here to know that quantities of goods at given costs are demanded at all. That is indicated by prices, without considering changing elasticity relationships or the differences of the relations between price of goods and desired quantities. *Prices may therefore be defined, in general,[27] as the marginal costs of quantities of goods demanded by consumers at these costs.** They are, so to say, prime costs, sanctioned by the consumer. This justifies appropriating means for their production up to the level of these sanctioned costs. The prices thus determined suffice entirely as guiding criteria to meet demands on producers.

At the same time, these justified costs accomplish everything that value indexes can to facilitate the preparation of the order of rank of demands for various goods. Insofar as the exchange relations within this order of rank have any significance at all, i.e., insofar as they are not completely fixed (and differences in urgency of needs are scarcely ever so great that in satisfying one it is possible to ignore another completely) all these purposes are reduced to a common de-

* Italics supplied by editor of translation.

nominator with the aid of costs. Thus, instead of comparing material needs elements with each other, it now becomes possible to make a thoroughgoing comparison of all these elements with the aid of a single measure. But this measure is not the "importance index" as such, if I may say so, for it *does not express differences in position in the order of rank of needs.** It rather expresses the systematization of exchange relations as cost indexes, i.e., alternatives, facing the consumer in choosing. It represents a system of uniform relative quantities with which individual aims can be achieved and goods be weighed after comparing their relative importance with each other. It thus becomes easier to see in how far items equally appraised and having the same costs are to be assigned varying significance. This facilitates segregating the large area of needs which, in this comparison, obviously appear more important, and hence require no closer consideration, i.e., which are distinctly intramarginal. At once it becomes apparent which items are in the marginal sector in which decisions become difficult. It establishes this border area, for here utility and cost value do not even coincide approximately. It is particularly useful where a basic need can be satisfied in various ways, by different products of equal or similar potential usefulness; and these are the decisions that involve choice most nearly alike, among means of production for the production of a good. Again we see that the price system *does not express the internal structure of the hierarchy of aims** of consumers; it *merely sets its limits.** In so doing it accomplishes its purpose fully, for the internal structure of the hierarchy is a matter of indifference for the guidance of production.

This assertion, however, needs a supplement. The internal structure of the hierarchy of aims of the consumer,

* Italics supplied by editor of translation.

the intramarginal significance of goods for him, for the time being, becomes important for production if conditions of production deteriorate, so that current effective demand can no longer be satisfied. It is then that this intramarginal importance of goods becomes apparent, in that demand is either fulfilled even at the necessary higher prices or allowed to go unfulfilled. The internal structure of the order of rank, which in general remains latent, becomes apparent from time to time in consumer price reactions. This is important, for it again suggests that correspondence between this hierarchy of purposes of consumers and measures taken by producers does not depend on the proportions of the price system as such, as would be the case *if they reproduced the entire order of rank,** but must be preserved by constant *supplemental reactions of consumers.**

In summing up, it may be said that the material order in rank of aims and goods is not converted, *as such,** into a financial valuation system. It rather remains a self-contained cosmos of successively balanced material choices. Outwardly it appears primarily as a system of decisions as to quantities. The externally corresponding relationship established between it and the financial valuation system of prices depends on the one hand on the fact that, from the side of those making choices, a certain but not strict relation exists between the exchange relations of goods, established by prices, and the selected assortment. On the other hand, on the side of producers there is a necessary relation between the composition of the assortment of goods produced and its production costs, i.e., its prices. If, therefore, demanded and supplied quantities of goods coincide at prevailing prices, the prevailing price system is thereby approved, from the side of demand.

* Italics supplied by editor of translation.

The significance of the financial valuation system consequently does not lie as much in the clarification of procedure in making the original choice of purpose (coordination of goals) which it merely facilitates by making certain data available but rather it lies primarily in conveying to the producers the results of the selection procedure by assembling the decisions of the individual participants in that selection, and in making possible the correct coordination between means of production and given goals, thus assuring optimal success in all stages of production (coordination of means). For this last purpose it is particularly indispensable.[28] The actual area of applicability of the financial valuation system is thus the production economy.[29]

For determining goal by the central authority the same must pertain as was just established for the choice of goal by the individual consumer. The actual problem is material. The choice among alternative purposes can be made here as well as there only in the material sense, in the form of immediate specific comparison of individual goals. If therefore material planning methods have considerable importance in determining goal by the state, this is nothing that distinguishes it from choice of goal by the private user.[30] It is here merely more pronounced, because of the greater scope of the task, since in the choice by the consumer the material part of the guiding process takes place in the individual head and does not become visible externally.

The scope of the posed coordination problem presents a fundamental peculiarity for the planning method. The accomplishment of the coordination process depends entirely on one head. Consistent coordination means that each separate opinion is made to coincide with all others. These separate opinions cannot be obtained as such because they cannot be expressed numerically. Furthermore, since an either fixed or derived opinion provides no adequate comparative data to measure specific or conceived purposes and needs, such coordination can be accomplished only by someone who has expressed these opinions and who can rely on his memory and imaginative power constantly to provide relevant conceptions anew. Hence a consistent coordination of all decisions as to choice is possible only if one head can comprehend and supervise this entire area of coordination and visualize all relevant components.

In the choice by consumers, the coordination areas are generally small so that to a certain extent it is possible to visualize them.[31] It is here a question of a multiplicity of such areas in which everyone is complete master in making decisions, the relative importance of which are determined by the extent of income, and which, moreover, are completely coordinated (*völlig gleichgeordnet*).

In determining the goal by the state, on the other hand, there is a coordination problem of such magnitude that it vastly exceeds the imaginative and coordinating power of one head.[32] The participation of numerous heads, indeed very many, in its solution cannot be avoided. Some method of dividing up the total problems must be found that will not harm the required comparison of immediately commensurable concepts[33] in the limited area assigned to one head, and yet, for all individual decisions in the entire area, at least an immediate, rough coordination will remain. The procedure to meet these requirements must so break down individual purposes and goals and assemble them into purpose groups and complexes that the assortment of purposes finally remaining becomes comprehensible to the heads[34] conducting the highest coordination. The global purpose and goal presentations thus assembled must again be made specific for the subordinate agencies in individual areas, in a hierarchical substructure gradually branching out. This must be differentiated to the point where the lowest agencies in their areas can supervise the individual purposes in their concrete formation. All these agencies participate in such initial material decisions of choice as components of the one guiding body which, as a whole, makes material decisions of choice as does every individual consumer.

As can be seen, the relation between the higher and lower agencies is the aggregative (global) described above. To determine the goal that is in the public interest, a guiding apparatus similar to that previously explained is required. The focal point of the material-guiding method is material-balancing. It merely requires that the apparatus created for the one problem—with corresponding extension —is transferred to the other, and herein lies a distinct connection between central determination of goal and material method of guiding. However, it is more of an accidental nature, and we must not overlook the fact that the fundamental problem in these cases is different. In the former it is a question of determining goals; the apparatus deals primarily with "goods of first order." The problem is expressed in every planning system in material terms. Actually, therefore, there is no competition between material and financial guiding methods.[35] The second problem, on the other hand, pertains to the allocation of means of production for given ultimate goals, the disposal of "goods of higher order." For this, to be sure, both material and financial methods of solution have been developed. Here a competition of methods, a conflict between them, might be possible. Whether this takes place will be examined in the following section. Differences in the problem again correspond with differences in the relations between higher and lower agencies. In the first case, the primary impulse comes from the higher agencies, and they are faced with the actual problems of forming models. In the second case, final data come from the lower agencies; the higher agencies merely have the problem of balancing.

The relation between higher and lower agencies in determining goal is, however, two-sided. On the one hand, lower agencies do not visualize the aggregate meaning of the purposes they decide. They judge the relative significance of the individual partial goals within the total perimeter delimited for them by the higher authority on the basis of the global estimate of the significance of the goal complex in its over-all setting. On the other hand, the opinion of the higher agencies, judging the over-all effect, is based on data provided by the lower agencies. Global conceptions of goal, serving as the basis for judging by the higher agencies, frequently enough attain their meaning only as aggregates of a multiplicity of individual problems recognized by the lower agencies and reported upward. At all events, the extent of the problem can be delimited only with this aid of the findings of the lower agencies, and these findings require independent collaboration if they are to be fruitful. Furthermore, the opinion as to the relative importance of individual goals and the goal complex requires knowledge of the exchange relations among them, i.e., knowledge of the extent to which one purpose must be abandoned, if it is desired to realize an additional goal of definite magnitude. But the costs are here not given independently of the choice of decisions made; they must be made available in the course of the planning process, on the basis of the choices made. Their determination can come only from the lower agencies in the coordinating process. The procedure of goal determination therefore does not develop *one-sidedly,** by gradually differentiating globally prescribed goals into individual tasks, but higher and lower agencies *jointly** achieve the entire system of goal-setting in a complicated process of mutual interaction.

It is impossible to deduce how initiative in determining goal shapes up in detail; how far the central agency follows the stimuli given it from below; how far it is able to draw the lower agencies into its drafts and induce them to participate actively in them. Here many alternative situations are possible. In general it may be established that wherever a long recognized need is to be further developed continuously, it will depend primarily on the initiative of the lower agencies, for they alone have knowledge of possibilities and difficulties. On the other hand, when radical changes in the structure of the needs are contemplated, when entirely new wants are to be satisfied or entirely new ways are to be found to satisfy them, the new draft must be drawn up by the central authority and transmitted to the lower agencies. The tendencies to schematize will be particularly strong here, because the central authority is forced to make binding its conceptions of the activities of the lower agencies and because the central agency is naturally able to recognize the new purpose, which is diversified in itself but extremely simplified. A particular case of such schematizing in the Soviet Union is the inclination to giant projects. For the central authority the giant project is the best understandable method of realization of purpose. Here purpose and method of realization are least differentiated. The purpose remains in the global form in which it has been conceived. The phenomena as to the internal structure

* Italics supplied by editor of translation.

whereby it may be realized shift very strongly from those economically realizable to those technically realizable. In like manner, there is also a certain tendency to proceed thus in the selection of purposes than can be realized as giant project units, such as canals, irrigation projects, giant power plants, and battleships. The lumped tasks or possibilities can be better visualized by the central authority than by widely distributed detailed work. But this is naturally only a tendency. It finds its particular justification in that, with reduction in the number of agencies making independent decisions, the central authority makes itself more independent of the uncertain initiative of these agencies, and hence more certain of its own successes.

The question that must be raised grows out of the relation of this material coordinating apparatus to the financial magnitudes which, as stated, are indispensable from the optimum view to guide production and furthermore, out of the position that financial magnitudes can and may eventually assume in the coordinating apparatus serving the choice of goal.

Financial magnitudes[36] enter the planning process, exactly as in the case of determining the goal by consumers, as marginal costs of the demanded quantities of goods resulting from the coordinating process. These marginal costs, to be sure, are not data for those making choices but, as indicated above, are dependent on the agreed quantity decisions, since here as in the case of consumer choice the influence of marginal costs cannot be neglected.[37] This further complicates the problem of planning. But there is here no basic difference, since every decision as to quantity has definite marginal costs ascribed to it. Rather, the process of choice of goal and the allocation of means of production—the choice of combinations of production means—can logically continue to be strictly separated.[38]

The marginal costs ascertained for individually planned items are then assembled into global indexes, even as in the case of the dependent goal units and partial goals. Thus there are at every stage of the planning hierarchy varying aggregate goal complexes, besides aggregate cost indexes. But the following difference results: goal complexes attain their form by cooperating between central and subordinate agencies, and the central authority has the actual problem of drafting the plan; on the other hand, the cost indexes of the upper agencies are secondary when compared with those of the lower agencies. Accordingly, they cannot be determined independently by the higher agencies. This is in accordance with the preceding interpretation. Financial magnitudes in the choice of goals are always the result of appropriate determination of quantity.

The resultant cost prices are not the same as indicators of the volume of output, as are corresponding prices reflecting consumer choice, and are not intended as such to the same extent. In setting the goal by consumers, prices are the index of volume of output for producers. The producer does not find out directly how much is to be produced, but derives this from prevailing prices and their changes. It does not depend on a different behavior of those setting the goal. As indicated, the private consumer in the first instance makes quantity decisions, even as does a choosing state agency.[39] Only price performs the task of obtaining for producers the results of all individually determined quantities, and they assess the result at their own risk. The choosing state agency, on the other hand, in general determines this total need immediately; price is therefore not the primary obligatory magnitude for producers, but quantities to be produced. Price therefore becomes a secondary magnitude, which is set in the planning process but does not regulate determination of quantity. This difference in the function of price arises, as indicated, not from differences in the guiding system, not from differing behavior of individual buyers, but from difference in the relation of buyer to producer. A large-scale buyer will always find himself in this position relative to the producer, no matter if it is the state or, for example, a private concern. This situation occurs frequently in a market economy, where the state appears as large buyer.[40] The result, however, is that material magnitudes take precedence over financial magnitudes in the guiding mechanism.

This is true, however, of final products only. For the production of intermediary products, prices can retain their status as regulators of quantity. Beyond that, they may also become effective as such in the area of placing of orders by influencing the producer's interest in the orders. This may affect the speed of processing and even lead to the attempt to reject individual orders, particularly if conditions of production, namely prices and available quantities of means of production, change subsequently.

This leads to the conclusion—which brings this trend of thought to an end—that the central authority, determining goals, has reasons for excluding this function of prices positively as regulator of quantities. This finally relates to possible varying reaction of buyer with changing conditions of production and deviations in resultant supply or output from what was expected. It is dependent on the extent of the coordinating area. In determining choice by the individual consumer, every buyer constantly visualizes the important basic requirement necessary for making his decision, and hence is constantly able to change his mind.[41] That is why it is possible for him, in choosing, always to consider existing supply. If output should decline, and hence also the possibility of realizing individual objectives, he will at once indicate those more important to him by maintaining his demand for these in spite of higher price. Thus the intramarginal meaning of purposes and goods, which cannot be derived directly from prices, appears in his reactions as soon as it becomes pronounced.[42]

If, on the other hand, as described above, several agencies participate in the coordinating process, they must be activated successively on the basis of the support and directives given by the others. Changes in output become apparent among the lower agencies that have immediate contact with the production apparatus. But the really important decisions must be made by the higher agencies, which alone have a perspective of the relative importance of all individual purposes and plans. They must then again be made specific by the lower agencies. A period of time elapses between the appearance of a change in growth and the completion of the new coordination of choices that becomes longer as the coordinating area becomes larger. Changes in conditions of production and hence in progress are to be expected constantly. To delay such change in the production process until a new decision has been reached would be impossible. It will not even be possible to set this extensive coordinating mechanism in motion to take account of every individual change. An adjustment and correction of setting of goal can occur only periodically.

Hence a constant difference between goals and results will appear in the guiding system, and this must be bridged by the lower agencies with preliminary decisions.[43] Because of constantly new appearance of difference, these decisions attain considerable importance with respect to the actual extent of fulfillment of different purposes. A way must thus be found that will assure their following the idea of the central authority as to the relative importance of individual goals. It may also be expressed thus: The given planning problem must be adjusted internally in accordance with the varying importance of the partial goals, since in its scope it cannot be constantly adjusted to changing conditions; the intramarginal significance of individual aims and goods must find expression in the proportions of the system itself, since it cannot be adequately expressed in the movements of the system.

This problem cannot be solved with the aid of financial magnitudes. This was previously explained in detail. But it is here necessary to return to it once more. Particularly for those thinking in terms of the market economy, the thought is somewhat intriguing that the state should make effective by gradations in the requisite money means[41] the different weights that it ascribes to the components of the program. For example, it should at the outset make available the requisite means for the armaments program or for provision of energy, so that at least the realization of the unconditionally essential item is assured. But this would be based on the idea that financial magnitudes could express the importance of goods and purposes independently of a selected total program, i.e., could express the intramarginal order of rank of purposes themselves. Actually, financial magnitudes have measurable effect only if they are aimed at a particular program, and this program must embody the originally planned assortment of purposes. Since prices function in relation to this assortment or at least correspond with it, they can no longer unfold meaningful effect if it is altered or cannot be fulfilled.

The only solution to the problem is to indicate the items in the adopted total plan that are of particular significance, where insistence on plan fulfillment is required even at the expense of total output. This indication must necessarily be material. It is possible in very rough form only, possibly by indicating the aggregate of purposes and within the aggregate those individual purposes that are to be given priority rating; in case of inadequate means, preference is given to those agencies responsible for fulfilling these purposes. In general, this again means that preferential treatment is given in the guidance system to material magnitudes over financial magnitudes.

This priority of material magnitudes does not merely pertain to determining final economic goals, to "goods of first order," but it pervades the entire production economy, directing means of production to given purposes. Purely financial guidance in the production sector leads to satisfactory results only under the assumption that equal sums of money express equal importance. This assumption, as shown above, is adequate for guiding production in that prices are recognized by those determining the goal by adhering to the quantity plan associated with them. But it does not hold if the quantity plans are upset. During the interval, until a new total coordination is accomplished, financial magnitudes are thus unreliable as directive criteria. The prevailing priority of specific purposes, established in material terms, must also be carried out in a material way in production.

Particular situations may give rise to further reasons for prevalence of material guidance methods. A financial guidance system requires time for adaptation. Every major shift in conditions of production or in the composition of established goals disrupts all the relationships on which its meaningful effectiveness depends. With independent producers, enormous frictional profits and losses appear, which subsequently decline faster or slower, depending on elasticity of conditions of supply. At all events, all bases of calculation first become null and void, and the new system of guidance can be reconstructed only gradually. The material guidance system, on the other hand, permits direct attack on set goals. For transition periods it can thus assure, if not optimal use of production possibilities, at least immediate exertion of all efforts directed toward the new goals, in the light of changed possibilities.[45]

Likewise, in such situations the central agency will not succeed in maintaining full control of the money means. This is because of the just-established fact that complete and orderly coordination of the system, particularly relative to measuring financial magnitudes, is impossible. Of more practical importance is the mood of the people. The attempt is made to deceive them as to the effects of the new situation on their living standard by maintaining their nominal status, even though the material basis for its maintenance no longer exists.[46] But as soon as uncontrolled sums of money appear in the system, productive (*fruchtbar*) financial guidance is no longer possible. The nonrecognized aims furthered with the aid of these sums cannot be distinguished financially from those that are acknowledged.

We conclude that a specific relation actually exists between setting of goal by the central agency and the application of material guidance methods. This relation is not based on a particular coordinating procedure nor on other intentions as to the nature of the desirable coordination. With basically similar interpretation of the coordinating problem, it is rather exclusively the result of the size of the coordination area and the associated changing reaction possibility of the coordination mechanism. That is why the ensuing material part of the coordinating process, occurring in goal determination in many heads of individual users, is manifested in an extensive guiding apparatus. On the other hand, since it is impossible to permit intramarginal importance of purposes and goods always to become effective by continuous reactions in the system, it now becomes necessary to consider them by fixing material priorities in the system itself.

But it is here not a question of a necessary relationship. Even with centralized setting of goal, a purely financial system of guidance is conceivable. It is conceivable, for example, that the central agency determines the sums of money at the highest coordinating stage in global (lump-sum) amounts for the separate goal complexes, and permits individual subordinate agencies to obtain the best possible results with these means in their areas of responsibility. But that would mean abandoning actual coordination of the assigned tasks and replacing them by a model, for it cannot be predicted to what extent individual aims can be achieved with these means, but only after coordination has been carried out systematically in the entire area. Moreover, abandoning completion of the entire plan by setting priority goals would leave an important group of decisions to chance. Financial criteria no longer operate in terms of the set goals if the bases of coordination change; their effective direction is now determined by accidentally apportioned financial credits and debits, resulting from shifts in conditions of production. Thus abandoning the material penetration of the guidance system means abandoning the realization of maximum success in terms of the given aims, even as would be the case of abandoning financial guidance with consumer freedom of choice and enterpriser freedom in the area of guiding production.

On the other hand, it is here not a question of an exclusive relationship, for financial magnitudes do not become superfluous as a result of material priorities. As indicated, guidance of means of production and attaining the desired goods from maximization views is possible only with the aid of financial guidance methods. This also continues if the guiding mechanism, aimed at assuring priority of specific goals, is carried out with material combinations. For these are merely intended to safeguard these goals against accidental detrimental shifts in the guiding system. But they cannot replace the optimum calculus; for optimum calculations financial magnitudes continue to be the standard. They are limited in their significance only insofar as goal or means substitution cannot be undertaken, when they hit upon such material combinations, even if they appear advantageous financially. And they contain a constant margin of error, since determining quantities on which ultimate financial magnitudes are based have meanwhile been surpassed in part. But that does not impair their usefulness, for an optimum calculation affected by unavoidable errors and limited in its effects is better than complete abandoning of efforts at maximization.

Compatibility of the Material and the Financial Guiding Method

This brings us to a discussion of the question with which our deliberation began: How may material and financial methods of guidance be combined in one system? This question, in a certain sense, is the central problem of a planned economy, for on the one hand material guiding methods, as here determined, are the actual significant new possibilities on which rests the claim to technical superiority of economic planning. That is why *competitive** socialist concepts are not entirely convincing; for abandoning these possibilities is hardly conceivable in a planned economy. This is particularly true of planned economies arising out of predominantly public setting of goal, as for example planned economies to overcome acute shortages or to change radically the economic structure[47] from which, as just shown, the material elements cannot be removed without injuring the system. On the other hand, abandoning the financial valuation system would mean abandoning effectiveness, from the point of view of performance, of striving to maximize, which would be such a weighty objection to any planned economic system that theoreticians therefore endeavor to develop a planned, socialistic economic system that foregoes material guidance methods.

Viewed as equilibrating methods, material and financial guidance are obviously absolute antitheses. In one case, the firm itself creates the balance by relating input and output quantities to the financial magnitudes prevailing in the market; in the other case, balance and hence the extent, at least in broad outline, of quantities of product and consumption are prescribed from above. One method is thus based on that freedom of choice of the immediate agency, guiding production, that is limited extensively by the other. But this does not imply that, in this connection, the important element in the financial method, i.e., the occasional achievement of equilibrium provided by the financial valuation

* Italics supplied by editor of translation.

system, cannot be integrated as such with the material guidance method. The inability to combine the two methods would have to be proved specifically.

The question may first be raised whether a material system of guidance must basically determine quantities of product other than a financial one. That is not the case. We must consider the setting of goals as given in both cases. Moreover, the material guiding method only induces the condition of equilibrium, as previously described; it establishes, as it were, partial material balances in all "producers' goods markets" (in the traditional sense). Such conditions of equilibrium are also a result of financial guidance. So far there is no contradiction between the two methods of guidance.

The equilibria striven for by the financial guidance system are then determined more accurately, in that they are related to an over-all optimum attainment of given final goals; thus, from the multiplicity of possible material balances, a definite one is selected. Such a closer determination is not connected with the material method of guidance by the system; it can rather produce arbitrary methods of balance. The financial method of guidance thus results in a closer determination of a condition of equilibrium, which is left indefinite by the material method. If, however, an optimum achievement of objective is likewise sought by the material method of guidance, it means a closer determination of the condition of equilibrium in the same direction in which financial guidance takes place; for the optimal condition is determined entirely by the order of rank of goals and the bases of production. The difference between the results of the two systems of guidance lies in the fact that conditions of equilibrium created by material guidance represent only a very rough approximation of the optimum.

In general, the financial guidance method is distinguished from the material method only as to the results produced, in that the former more nearly approaches the optimum principle that the material method of guidance is seeking to attain.

The objection to the compatibility of the material method of guidance with the application of the financial valuation system thus can only be based on the assumption that the financial valuation system cannot be established reliably by employing the material method of guidance. When applying the financial method of guidance, precision in establishing correct relations in the financial valuation system depends on the fact that the individual concern is induced by interest in financial success to relate quantities of product and outlay to financial valuation of these magnitudes in the market, and that consequently material disequilibria will remain until general coordination of material and financial magnitudes has been achieved throughout the entire economy. Such a situation, which does not permit the economy to come to rest until it has attained optimal balance and actually has been forced to it, does not pertain when applying the material method of guidance, for eliminating material disequilibria is the first direct point of attack in the planning process.

However, this objection is effective only if material disequilibria are the only means by which final optimal and comprehensive equilibrium can be brought about. Undoubtedly the way to a complete condition of equilibrium moving toward an optimum may be achieved (1) by equating price and marginal cost with price and marginal product (with the aid of supply and demand quantities) by means of a material supply and demand balance. Conversely, it may also be achieved (2) by creating a balance between produc-

tion and consumption (balancing) and subsequently changing the level of this initial material balance by determining,
with the aid of marginal-cost-and-product computation,
the direction in which it shall be developed further toward
an optimum. Thus, for example, marginal costs of every
product at given prices of means of production and marginal products of the means of production at given product
prices, likewise basic trends, with changes in quantities of
output and input, can be calculated and added to the basic
tables for material balances of volume of production and
consumption. Observed changes in trend in the composite
balance would then be indicated in abbreviated rough
form, so that they may be considered in the shifts and cur-
tailment needed to achieve balance and also to test the ad-
visability of further shifts. For example, low marginal costs
relative to price would indicate that at this point production can be advantageously expanded; relative high marginal products of a means of production would indicate that
major emphasis could be shifted to this product by appropriate shifts in the combination of means of production.
The lower coordinating agency would have to test whether
it can improve conditions of equilibrium by alterations
in its area. Insofar as this is not the case, it reports in addition to its composite balance sheet the reserves of low-cost
expansion of output and need for shifts in requirements:
greater need for certain means of production and lesser need
for others. The next higher agencies proceed in like manner. The highest agencies then determine for what products
there is particular need for the entire economy and wherever
favorable expansion of production is possible at low cost,
and take this into account by considerably expanding production of goods for which at the time there is particular
need in this sense (high marginal products at many places)

and for which the possibility of low-cost production expansion exists. Furthermore, for goods with particular need, output is expanded at once and prices are raised, while for goods with favorable possibilities of expansion (low marginal cost relative to price) prices are lowered and ultimately production is expanded. Finally, for goods the use of which it is desirable to restrict (which show relatively low marginal products) production is contracted, and in some cases prices are lowered [apparently this should read "raised"].[48]

The major objections to this method relate to inadequate elasticity. On the one hand, the number of possible combinations is so great that their computation to carry out complete economic coordination is inconceivable, while the gropings of all separate units trying out the various possibilities on their own account allow the total process to converge in the direction of the optimum. On the other hand, it is this experimentation that as trial-and-error testing method, according to the assumptions of the supposed theory of our market economy as well as in the model of competitive socialism, first allows the determining of cost and yield functions. By applying the method here presented, there is no occasion for such experimental inquiry, since coordination is achieved mathematically in advance. But generally too much weight is put on the significance of experimentation (trial and error) in seeking the optimal combination; in practice enterprises are accustomed to be far more inelastic in their production policies than our theory assumes, and in particular, in the majority of cases, combinations of means of production actually permit far less room for variations. Thus the purely statistical determination of yield and cost functions that finds support in many-sided individual experience may not be altogether unjustified. And the same holds true for experimentation (trial and error) in establishing equilibrium. Furthermore, as is known, it is not necessary that the entire process should converge with simultaneous variation of its components; diverging and cyclical developments are known in theory as well as in practice. They primarily result because, through inadequate surveying of the over-all situation, the individual concern is misled in its adjustment policies by the results of mistaken trial-and-error policies of other concerns remaining in the market. Finally, it is not certain to what extent the centrally directed guiding process need necessarily be inelastic; it is conceivable that it be made elastic by more frequently inserting correctional measures.

It will at least be possible to establish the fact that the thoroughness with which the two partial problems are solved in realizing perfect equilibrium differs for the two methods of attaining equilibrium. Each method achieves something better with the partial problem that it first attacks directly. Thus the approach of marginal costs and marginal revenues to prices will be carried further with purely financial guidance. This is because of greater elasticity in the condition of production than in a guidance system in which every change in production must first be made to balance with all changes that have taken place in other enterprises. By way of contrast, achieving a material condition of equilibrium remains more problematical here and the adverse effects owing to unsuitability (misdirected production and investments) are the chief disturbing factors that continue to negate successes in fulfilling the initial partial tasks. These ill effects become greater the longer the period of adjustment necessary for management to make them effective in the market. Most obvious are, therefore, the defects of purely financial guidance in the area of long-term investment planning, where material complementarity of the measures cannot be remotely assured. The material method of guidance has particular significance here, since, in turn, it can carry out material balance by also considering the temporal disposal of quantities of product with reasonable certainty, but only roughly approximate balance of marginal revenues and marginal costs and prices.[49]

These reflections are not intended to prove with calculated precision the superiority of either the one or the other coordinating system. Such proof cannot be provided by a purely deductive analysis. It was here merely intended to show that there is no reason for overemphasis on the imperfections of the coordinating process and its results in planned economic "centralized" guidance. The coordinating process in a market economy likewise reveals many weighty imperfections, and nothing further can be proved for either of the two guidance systems than that it is constantly possible to create tendencies anew from within toward the optimal equilibrium viewpoint without ever attaining it.

We arrive at the conclusion that the material guidance method and the construction of a financial valuation system theoretically are by no means mutually exclusive, and that their actual combination in a guidance system, with sufficient practical results, is at least conceivable. On the other hand, a certain amount of tension as to the question of control remains unresolved. The material system of guidance and control, as shown, is based on graduated limitation of the area of exchange. Financial methods of control cannot guarantee adherence to these gradations, but rather mislead to illegal penetration of these barriers by discovering additional advantageous exchange opportunities. But this defect loses much of its significance if the financial valuation system is consistently coordinated since, to that extent, the occasion for such disruption of the material guidance system disappears.

The Position of the Enterprise in the Soviet Guiding System

Insofar as the relationship of material and financial planning is concerned, the possible conformity of the two methods of guidance has not been realized in the Soviet Union. This conformity can result consciously only from an insight into the meaning and condition of both planning methods. But there it is intended, in accordance with conscious setting of goal, to realize a purely material planning system in which money accounting merely aids as instrument of control. Thus the influence of financial criteria appears only in "roundabout" manner, out of the logic of the situation, which becomes visible and effective in individual cases but cannot consistently permeate the entire system. And so it happens that the *higher planning agencies** practice a purely *material** guidance system, while the influence of *financial guiding** criteria applies only to the *lowest** units, the enterprises.

But this results in that conflicting situation between material and financial guidance which, according to Western critics of economic planning, is unavoidable,[50] but which, as shown, would be entirely avoidable with correct synthesizing of the two planning systems. Excepting for its own influence on formulating the plan, to be discussed later, the enterprise has production goals prescribed for it as well as basic proportions of material combination of means, possibly with some flexibility. It endeavors to break these material fetters here and there, motivated by financial con-

* Italics provided by editor of translation.

siderations and influenced by guiding financial criteria.

The fundamental tie (*Bindung*) of enterprises to the material planning problems and permitted means (*Mittelvorgaben*) is constantly emphasized. Evidence of this was cited previously.[51] "Operative independence" is afforded them only in the sense that they are permitted to accomplish the requisite task with less expenditure and, with the aid of the given bases of production, to achieve a larger total output while observing requisite assortment conditions. "In a planned economy, operative economic independence can be permitted only within the limits and on the basis of the economic plan, for the purpose of fulfilling and overfulfilling planned tasks in the interest of the entire economy. The independence of the State socialistic *khosraschet* enterprises consists of giving them the right, by disposing of public means assigned to them and using all their internal possibilities, to seek and to select the best ways and methods to attain the set goals, the best ways and methods to fulfill and overfulfill the planned tasks," [52] whereby also "exceeding planned input norms" represents a violation of the plan.[53] The separate enterprise is normally to produce a materially fixed (least) quantity of product, with a given plant capacity, from a materially fixed (maximal) expenditure of means of production (including labor). The prices of products and of means of production (including wages) are likewise fixed. Sale of products and provision of production means, as such, are not included in their tasks, but are assigned to special agencies, directly subordinate to the higher economic management.[54]

This strict tie, as shown in the preceding chapter, could not be maintained. Rather it became necessary to permit enterprises more or less freedom of choice as to a part of these decisions and functions whereby they were to be bound by the plan. This practical loosening or abolishing of the ties may be achieved in various ways. On the one hand, it may be that the absolutely desired connection, finding expression in corresponding planned tasks, can simply not be realized, so that management finds itself in a continuous, frequently unsuccessful conflict with the transgressors. That may go so far that one must speak of actual impossibilities of carrying out the obligations; the instructions of the plan thus attain the character of mere directives, "progress." The final step is the official abandonment of such ties, the legally sanctioned release from them. Furthermore, loosening of the ties must take into consideration that enterprises themselves participate in drawing up the plan and thereby can influence the planned task assigned to them.

The extent of the effective ties and the manner of loosening them are very different in separate planning areas. Complete understanding of the Soviet guidance system could be obtained only by a detailed investigation of these changing connecting relationships.[55] I can here merely compile what I have found at points of contact to judge the question, which may perhaps give an idea of the varied possibilities of the situation, but voice no definite opinion as to its weight within the framework of the over-all arrangement.[56]

The intended tie (*Bindung*) is expressed by fixing production goals in the plan, including the manner of their fulfillment, together with the requisite material expenditure. The economic activity of enterprises is extensively engaged in this planned task as well as in the report of its fulfillment. However, this relationship is incomplete. It must first be pointed out that it is impossible to attain that complete mutual agreement with the aid of the material planning and balancing system that would be necessary if it were desired to achieve integration of enterprises. As shown in the first chapter, "Participation of Central and Lower Agencies in Drawing Up of the Plan," planning passed through the following stages: first, equilibrium of input and output quantities was temporarily prepared for the entire economy, in which the relationship of volume of product and material expenditure was estimated only approximately for separate production processes, with the aid of lump-sum norms; thereupon this relationship was recomputed and reported by separate enterprises in drawing up their own production plan; finally aggregate input and output quantities were balanced anew, on the bases of these corrected figures and the necessary reallocations undertaken, which appropriately were then considered in the plans of the separate enterprises.

This procedure has an unavoidable defect in that it is based on the temporary allotments to the lower units, which are corrected in the subsequent planning process. This defect becomes the more apparent the cruder the lump-sum norms are, with the aid of which the first draft of the plan was drawn up, and the less they are able to realize the actually attainable relationship of input and output. Indeed, there is considerable complaint that the initial production plans, on the basis of which enterprises begin to operate, and in particular establish their input requirements, deviate sharply from the final planned tasks.[57]

Furthermore, the planning process evidently does not become specific enough in fixing required intermediary allotted items for specific projects. Separate enterprises rather obtain their allotted supplies for their planned tasks —even if more specific—in terms of lump-sum norms. For example, it is reported that for the building industry the material demands are not based on worked-out plans, but are computed from composite index numbers expressing the relationship of certain items of expenditure to sum total costs of the buildings. "In practice . . . building organizations in October merely receive a general quota, in the form of a value figure, for their expenditure in the coming year. Orders for material and equipment, which they submit at this time, must therefore depend on average relative proportions for requirements of materials, expressed in millions of rubles of costs, based on experience and expectation of individual branches of the building industry; they therefore do not appear to be precise enough." [58] Similar procedures are also met in other branches of industry.[59]

For all these reasons the plan as drawn up cannot be viewed as completely obligatory from the beginning. It is rather necessary from the beginning to consider that the need for this or that item of input will deviate from that estimated, and that therefore enterprises will, on the one hand, make their supplementary need for input supplies known and, if not met, will not fulfill their assigned production; and, on the other hand, are capable of accumulating surpluses of such input items.

More aggravating is the fact that, because of its cumbersomeness, the planning process in the Soviet Union is regularly not completed on time, and that therefore enterprises regularly receive their obligatory plans only after considerable delay, possibly several months later. This simply results in reduced production, where enterprises are absolutely dependent on these plans, in order to be able to do anything. That is, for example, often the situation in the building industry, where work during the first quarter of the year is delayed considerably by failure of plans.[60] Moreover, it must serve as an appeal to the individual initiative of enterprises that in the meantime have to work according to noncorrected plans, and cannot be held responsible, in like manner, because of their extensive independent action.

In other respects enterprises also have considerable influence over adjusting their planned tasks themselves. This pertains to the scope of the planned tasks. Again and again the complaint is heard that enterprises know how to provide an "easy plan" for themselves. The possibility of doing this is provided primarily by their influence on determining norms. The significance of norms for setting possible production results and requisite expenditure derives from what was said in the first chapter, and the bases for setting these norms originate in the performance of separate enterprises, so that they themselves provide the standard of performance to be required of them.

The system of progressive norms and plans to lower costs, with the aid of which this relationship is established and enterprises are forced to raise their standards, is presented in the first chapter. But it must here be pointed out that in this respect enterprises are actually not controlled as intensively as would seem necessary. Thus complaints are heard that enterprises arbitrarily raise their input norms and thereby ease their cost status—and naturally their planned tasks at the same time. "But cases are still found where some enterprises raise their requirements of material, in drawing up their planning estimates, by increasing their expenditure norms as well as wage sums, by increasing labor requirements for products and needed wage rates, and by including unnecessary extras for deviations from the technological process, whereby finally administrative and operational overhead costs are increased." [61] To illustrate: "Planned costs of a turn screw lathe for 1951, produced in the machine-tool factory at Tiflis, were raised 10%, by an unwarranted increase of expenditure for cast iron for a lathe in the planning division of the factory by 30%, and expenditure for wrought iron by 29%. In the foundry Petrovskij the norm for fuel input for producing cast forms, in 1951, was set at 272 kg. (per ton) although in 1950 the factory used only 200 kg. per ton. The actual fuel input amounted to only 193 kg. in 1951." [62] "In factories producing electric machinery even today the inadmissible practice pertains of setting contradictory norms. One norm is set for material requirements, another is used for this same material or product in determining planned costs, and a third is used in allotting this material in the plant." [63]

The defective ability to control enterprises with reference to handling norms leads to the proposal to appeal to the self-interest of the lower agencies. "The main defect"—namely, the premium system—"consists almost exclusively of awarding premiums for overfulfilling the plan to lower costs and realize unplanned savings. This may, however, find expression, in that concerns and divisions do not reveal all given possibilities of lowering costs in drawing up the plan and, in some cases, advance a proposal for cost reduction, which is set too low." [64] However, this freedom in dealing with norms is naturally only a limited occurrence. In some respects the inability to control lower agencies goes much further. In some managerial areas they are not yet controlled by norms at all. "In several factories of the Ministry of Machine Tool Construction and at the Electric Industry Ministry, input norms are fixed only for metals and for several other basic materials. On the other hand, in some cases provision of norms for input of subsidiary materials, tools, fuel, electric energy, is lacking and hence the necessary control of their use in production does not exist." [65] The liberties taken relative to planned tasks per-

tain not only to norms and cost indexes but also to prescribed quantity of output itself. Thus Podšivalenko reports:
"In the course of the year 1951, the building trust program
of the crude oil industry in Čeljabinsk was often changed.
If the program of this trust is set at 100% on January 1, it
amounted to 92% on July 1, as a result of changes made in
the plan, to 89% on September 1, to 80% on October 1, to
78% on November 1, and at the end of the year to 76%." [66]
   Besides being able to influence the extent of their
planned task, enterprises can also influence its composition,
its "assortment." The planned task is frequently set for
them in more or less lump-sum form, and subsequently
broken down by them.[67] Nothing having general validity
can be said as to the degree to which enterprises are able
to specialize and the extent to which this is subsequently
included in the balance and corrected by higher-ups. In this
connection important symptoms are, on the one hand, the
complaints—coming from above or from the enterprises
themselves—of nonadherence to the fixed product mix provided in the plan, and on the other the attempts to influence the composition of these assortments with the aid
of price setting. These were both discussed in "Differing
Attitude Toward Use of Financial Magnitudes as Lead
Criteria" of the preceding chapter. They show clearly that
control of production results as to assortments is largely
ineffective. By way of supplement it should be observed
that there are areas in which production performance is not
prescribed in the plan, but where the initiative of enterprises is intentionally allowed free play of action (*Betäti-
gung*). Included here, for example, is production of consumers' goods from material remnants and waste discarded
in another production process that cannot be used other-

wise.[68] As parallel phenomena in the field of agriculture, domestic products of individual collective farm peasants appearing in the *kholkos* market might be mentioned.

These liberties in determining production tasks also pertain to those measuring input, in the nature of "demand" of a concern for means of production. Thus Sokolov speaks of the "arrangement to supplement basic means for building organizations": "In view of their dependency on the building program, special investment means are allotted to building organizations for the construction of buildings and for providing building machinery and means of transportation. For this purpose, advances are provided in general building cost estimates, usually up to 5 to 6 per cent of the entire estimate. These advances are transferred to the building organizations, regardless of the condition of the basic means, and on this depends the possibility of providing themselves with superfluous tools and equipment." [69] Here is the possibility of exercising relatively free and uncontrolled demand, with purely synthesized allocation of sums of money.

Disposal of product and provision of requisite input items must consistently be regulated by the plan as specifically as production itself, since production plans attain meaning and possibility of attainment only in their subsequent connection with the distribution network. Beyond this it is also expected that the distribution network will assist in the control of production, since adherence to the set production tasks relative to quantity and quality, as well as permissible expenditures, is not based on announcements and reports, but can be controlled effectively only in relation to the deliveries that have been made.[70] While material control is not fully effective in the production sector, even less is to be expected of it in the distribution sector, since the distribution system is more varied and extensive (*unübersicht-*

lich) because of many-sided ramifications of goods produced solely by one concern. Hence the centrally organized distribution network legally does not include all products, and not with equal intensity those that are included. A distinction is made among:

1. "Funded products" ("centralized fund") the detailed distribution of which is regulated according to distribution plans, naming recipients and consumption quantities, authorized by the Council of Ministries
2. Contingent or quota products ("regulated goods"); of these a quota is allotted in the plan to individual industries, trusts, and regions, and the operative branch of the producing ministry (*Glavky*) makes deliveries or allotments to individual orderers, until the quota of their industrial branch or their region is used up
3. "Decentralized products"; they are purchased directly by the users or by the purchase divisions of the ministries (*Glavsnab*) from the producers, mainly local industries, cooperatives, and agriculture[71]

Funded products, to be sure, embrace all important means of production and all mass consumers' goods.[72] Nevertheless, according to more recent statements,[73] "decentralized funds" represent 25 per cent of consumer goods sales and also include a part of important building materials and agricultural raw materials.[74] Concerning these it is no longer possible to speak of effective control of sale and supply. Relative to production and use of these goods enterprises are no longer subjected to actual delivery control, but only relative to statistical reports and to their financial system.

But material control is also imperfect relative to goods in

the first two groups. Here frequently the plan merely establishes the delivery terms. In the delivery and allotment of the goods themselves, higher agencies are only partially involved; otherwise it proceeds directly from enterprise to enterprise, with the aid of the previously explained system of planned contracts.[75] Mutual control of concerns, however, proceeds in financial form as shown, and only thus is it effective.

Beyond this, at all events, doubts must be expressed as to the effectiveness of these stipulated delivery relations for some areas. For this regulation of delivery obligations makes sense only insofar as an enterprise is held to fulfilling its task. If, however, carrying out of the planned task completely cannot be counted on anyway, because of inadequacy of its calculated bases, or if the enterprise itself is able to alter these subsequently, it must be concluded that it will be able to evade its delivery obligations even more.[76]

The other side of this easing of (*Lockerungen*) strict adherence to the plan is that to separate enterprises the guidance system cannot guarantee provision of those input items that they require to perform the planned task. This may easily lead enterprises into the pincers between planned task and procurement situation that will directly necessitate their violating some managerial regulations. The position of enterprises in this respect is described by Bienstock as follows:

> Since procurement is both planned and executed by higher organs, the role of plant manager is somewhat peculiar. He seems to lack all opportunity for action and still to be responsible for results, i.e., output. In theory higher agencies must supply plants with all necessary fuel, raw materials, semifinished goods and equipment, and

organize the sale of finished products. In practice, however, the plant manager must watch carefully lest the procurement plan not be carried out in time. To obtain goods, he must often send representatives to supplying factories or to agencies of People's Commissariats or *"glavks."* [77] Many plants have permanent representatives in Moscow or other supply centers with the special task of securing timely supply of goods, of pushing orders for materials, of arranging shipments, etc. . . . A plant manager who does not get needed goods in time is often compelled to break rules and seek new ways of supplying his plant. . . .

Selling is far easier. The manager sells his funded and quota products through higher selling organs. For goods of the decentralized category, above all for goods destined for ultimate consumption, he must study consumer needs, take the initiative, find buyers. Owing to the scarcity of commodities, however, Soviet producers are faced with no acute problem of finding a market.[78]

In consequence, regulating supply occasionally slips out of the hands of the state distributing apparatus altogether. Thus conditions develop similar to black markets, while enterprises in some cases proceed to produce on their own; both affect observance of the cost plans. Illustrations of this will be given in the following chapter. Insofar as this occurs, it can be said that the financial guidance system surmounts the material one. However, it is naturally once more only a matter of partial phenomena about whose importance in the total picture nothing certain can be established.[79]

The labor market has particular significance in this connection. Efforts have been made to bring it under control. The number of employees and allocated technical and office personnel are fixed in the plan, and with balances of labor forces, the effort is made to locate and direct supply of and demand for labor precisely. Recruiting of labor forces was legally regulated in detail. Until recently change of place of employment was possible only with approval of the employing enterprise. For a long time heavy penalties were imposed on workers and employees who changed jobs without approval, and for replacement of skilled personnel. Yet this did not succeed in bringing the movement of labor forces fully under control. Illegal change of place of employment remained a burning problem, and shortage of labor forces, particularly of trained, skilled labor, led enterprises not only to undertake recruiting contrary to regulations, but also to make positive efforts at piracy of skilled labor from each other.[80] Recently the free mobility of employees was again officially introduced.[81] All this means that the state also cannot guarantee to enterprises the provision of the necessary supply of labor to fulfill the plan, and in consequence a certain self-made legality results in the development of wages and hence costs, which in general finds expression in the formation of wage relations and in the dynamics of the money system.[82]

Now we finally come to the question as to who is responsible for setting prices. As such, this power is strictly centralized. In general, the highest government office, the Council of Ministers, is responsible for setting prices of the bulk of important producers' goods, intermediary products, and consumer goods as well as for agricultural delivery prices,[83] and the control is here very tightly drawn by detailed price lists. However, it does not include all goods. For a number of less important goods, industrial ministries set the prices; for products of local industry and of industrial producers' cooperatives, prices not set by them are set by the Council of Ministers of the Republics and the executive committees of the regions. Above all, of particular importance among the powers of ministers of industry is the setting of prices of newly introduced products—by agreements between the supplying and the purchasing ministry for a period of the first six months or until the item has been entered in the official price lists—and of processed goods custom made, to which the prices of official price lists are not applicable.[84] In all cases the price-setting authority may be delegated still further to chief administrations or even to the enterprises themselves. Ministries, as Majzenberg complains, make irresponsible use of this privilege, in that they extend it beyond the intended limits, and in so doing do not even exercise the requisite controls. Thus an area develops in which lower agencies, including even enterprises themselves, can set prices with relative freedom.[85]

But also for the other prices "confirmed by the Council of Ministers" this central price-setting does not mean as much as one might be led to believe. These price-settings also rest on the bases obtained from the ministries, and ultimately on the size of the processing expenditures in the enterprises. As shown above, enterprises can exercise decided influence on the formation of these bases, these norms. In addition, temporary price-setting of newly introduced products that have a particularly large influence on enterprises often serves as example for subsequent final price-setting. Thus confirmation of these prices by the central agency in the first instance affects their stability, but only conditionally their height. Individual arbitrariness is excluded by the uniformity of price-setting where presumably also a certain reluctance appears to exploit one's own influence too severely in this more easily controllable area. But naturally the central agency, in turn, is able to set these prices, deviating from these initial data provided by the lower agencies, if in so doing one wants to attain certain guidance results. Release from the stated bases (processing costs) permits these prices, which are actually very centrally set, to become a particularly rough guiding instrument.

When it finally comes to the above-mentioned conditions "similar to black markets," establishing terms of trade passes entirely into the hands of the immediate participants. Illustrations of this will again be given in "Significance of Inflation" in the following chapter. But naturally it is here merely an exceptional phenomenon. Most of industrial turnover presumably takes place in the legal manner at official prices.

Supplementing all these conclusions, it should be pointed out that where enterprises are obligated by the plan, this obligation need not always be carried out according to the intentions of the central authority. Intermediary agencies in the economic bureaucracy can also pursue self-interest, and complaints are frequently heard that this takes place. In this connection the position of chief administrations is particularly noteworthy. Here lies the greatest ability for control of enterprises but at the same time the strongest common interests with enterprises, as a result of concurrent responsibilities. Above all, chief administrations frequently receive a financial incentive directly. This is because profits and losses of enterprises subordinated to them are compiled in a composite balance sheet, and the state's withdrawal of profits and investment assignments together with resultant allocation of means from the State budget are related to the showing on this composite balance sheet. This goes so far that top administrations are spoken of subject to *khozra-schet*. Here therefore the next higher member of the economic bureaucracy can slip into a position relative to the plan similar to that of the enterprises. This is particularly significant in view of the very extensive functions of top administrations in planning distribution (disposal and procurement) and investments.[86]

Distribution of Influence in Planning Investments

Of particular interest in this connection is the manner in which competence and influence in investment planning are distributed. Here the idea of strict centralization pertains. Basically, exercise of independent action by enterprises in this area is forbidden. Without authorization they were permitted, until recently, to acquire equipment items only in exceptional cases, and then only to a value of not more than 300 rubles. Investment goods belong to the most rigorously managed class of goods, to funded products. Sale or exchange of parts of plants and equipment items without approval of the central agency is also strictly forbidden.[87]

However, this also is not unconditional. In order to delimit the possibility of exercising influence, it is required in the first place to outline briefly the system of investment planning relative to the participant agencies, as far as can be ascertained.

Setting goals for the investment program is derived from the relationship between the directives specified in the general economic goal setting and the available production bases, with the aid of the method of balances,[88] as shown in the first chapter. The fundamental lines are therefore established by the government, while *Gosplan* and the ministries provide the bases and undertake to work out details. It is, moreover, scarcely possible to estimate the distribution of the actual influence among government heads and the ministerial bureaucracy.

Drawing up of a project within the established framework, moreover, is the concern of the ministries. But diverse exercise of influence by the central agency is again reflected in the procedural regulating of authorization. Upper limit projects and lower limit projects are here distinguished. Upper limit projects are those where the cost estimates exceed a certain sum—the limit—varying from one branch of industry to another. They must be approved by the Council of Ministers of the USSR and for this purpose are assembled into lists of titles that indicate, among other matters, location, planned capacity, and estimated costs of the project, status of construction, and anticipated length of time before completion, as well as that required to put partial capacities into operation. Lower limit projects are approved by the qualified ministers within the limits of the total sums allotted to the ministry.[89] Authorization procedure by the Council of Ministers for larger projects, exceeding a certain sum, extends to planned tasks with the preliminary cost of calculations and, in case of very large and completely new types of undertaking, also to the entire technical project, together with main cost estimates.[90]

Moreover, besides planning divisions of the ministries, enterprises also participate in drawing up of projects, insofar as they pertain to extension projects and expansion of already existing enterprises. For this they are informed as to the limiting data for the project—capacity and fundamental, technical data—set forth in the plan, and within these limits they carry out individual adjustments and items of expenditures.[91] On the other hand, there are special projecting organizations which, on order from the ministries and possibly also from enterprises, make detailed technical and cost calculations where it is a case of an extensive undertaking.[92]

One influence of enterprises on investment planning

might possibly result from their participation in carrying out planning calculations. It may be safely assumed that they can exercise a certain influence; it is, as has been said, not possible to control the diversity of actions to be carried out, in detail, by the higher apparatus. On the other hand, this influence may not pertain to the really essential data. The nature and extent of capacity to be provided are fixed and observance of decisions in this respect is controllable from above. Hence any influence of enterprises on the development of production—which is the issue here considered—cannot be assumed as such, or at most only insofar as they can make suggestions in drafting the plan as to the direction in which capacity is to be developed further.

Next the question may be raised whether any peculiarities in division of influence are connected with the manner of raising investment means. The following sources of investment financing are distinguished in the Soviet Union:[93]

1. Allotments from the State budget, i.e., from the general tax sources.
2. Depreciation allowances, or a fixed quota of the same. The height of depreciation varies according to industrial branch, nature of the investment, and intensity of its use, expressed in terms of percentages of their original value, and is fixed by the Council of Ministers and the separate ministries; the average rates around which they move amount to 5 to 6 per cent depending on the industrial branch.[94] Of the sums thus realized, a part is put at the disposal of the respective enterprises for so-called major repairs of their plants— the quotas range between 40 per cent and 50 per cent, with a special allowance of 65 per cent for light in-

dustry;[95] the rest is turned over to the State and serves to finance new investments.

3. Actual profit of enterprises in whose field new investment takes place, or profits shared by their higher chief administration in this field.

4. Proceeds from the sale of superfluous or discarded plant parts, idemnifications, and insurances.

5. Means from "mobilizing internal reserves of building concerns" as well as those from "savings by lowering building costs."

The last mentioned items are in a certain sense particularly typical of the Soviet type of economic observation. The most important of these, "mobilization of internal reserves," relates, as such, to regulating working capital of building organizations, particularly their supply of materials and inventory of machinery; it is thus not merely a matter of freeing means, but also of supplemental tying up of means. The chief significance, as the name indicates, however, lies in the saving of means as a form of increasing output, and hence apparently other successes of related increases in performances are also included under this heading which, as causes of unplanned profit, actually belong under item 3.[96] The latter also holds for "savings by lowering building costs." That these items are here pointed out as special sources of financing is related to the technique of estimating costs. At the outset the fact is taken into account that cost-reducing reserves are included in the cost estimates of the planned calculation of items of expenditure from price and norm handbooks, which grant lump-sum extras,[97] and that the attempt is made subsequently to strike a balance by seizing these reserves.[98] However, they require no special treatment for the question raised here, such as specially computed and controlled elements of profit or working capital made liquid again, in comparison with other profit realized by the enterprise.

That part of profits must be segregated which is placed in the so-called directors' fund, i.e., the profits from the sale of consumers' goods that an enterprise produces, besides its planned assignment, in the so-called utilization divisions, from material remnants and waste products.[99] These means represent "own means" of an enterprise in a special sense. Their significance for investments will be discussed subsequently.

The remaining parts of profit must be paid to the State as a profits tax.[100] They represent public revenues at the disposal of the State for general purposes, even as do revenues from turnover tax, income tax, or other sources of income. The same is true of the other sources of investment financing, particularly of amortization. It is by no means self-evident that depreciation must be newly invested in concerns that charge it off; rather, liquidation of invested resources in the form of depreciation provides the natural opportunity to change the investment structure of the entire economy by permitting overexpanded branches relative to the over-all planned objective to contract gradually.

Profits and depreciation charges are actually treated in this manner, insofar as they cannot be invested on the basis of existing investment within the area of firms producing them. Withdrawals of profits represent an important item of income of the State budget. In 1941 they amounted to 14.3 per cent, and according to the estimate for 1954, to 16.2 per cent of the total revenue of the State budget.[101] In particular, profits and depreciation charges of consumer goods industries are extensively drawn on to finance investments in heavy industries.[102]

But also that part of profits provided for investment by the enterprises producing it and therefore not needing to be transferred to the State budget, as well as all means raised otherwise by enterprises for investment purposes—aside from those allotted to the special fund of enterprises—are clearly indicated as public funds. On the other hand, public investment plans decide whether investments take place in the area of enterprises or chief administrations that may provide these means, or whether they need be withdrawn for lack of such projects. On the other hand, even though they are invested in the area of enterprises and chief administrations, this takes place according to plans that have been drawn up by the economic bureaucracy and approved in accordance with established rules. Finally, these means are also turned over to *Prombank,* and in case of failure to pay them promptly, the bank seizes them and supervises their planned use.[103]

Nevertheless, these means are distinguished from allotments from the State budget, and are recorded as "own means" of enterprises. They are further distinguished as "localized" own means, i.e., depreciation charges and profits of the reinvesting enterprise itself, and centralized own means, i.e., depreciation charges and profits that accrue to the chief administration in the area of enterprises subordinated to it, and put at their disposal by it.[104] The limit to the withdrawal of profits is set so that first the planned requirement of investment means of the enterprise is covered, including planned additional need for working capital and contributions to the own funds of the enterprise, and only the remainder is paid into the State budget; conversely, only an unsatisfied need for investment means is covered by allotments from the State budget.[105] In general, the same procedure is followed relative to the chief administration.

The reason for this special treatment of "own means" is said to be that enterprises would become more interested in raising these means and hence in fulfilling their production and cost plans, since investments assigned to them can be carried out only insofar as planned depreciation charges and profits are actually realized.[106] It is thus assumed that merely defining the requirements in the plan is insufficient to induce enterprises to fulfill them, and that they have a greater interest than the State in carrying out investments and in increasing their capacity.[107]

A further reason for this contrasting may be found in the historical development of the planning system. It developed out of a condition in which enterprises extensively provide the initiative also for investments, and largely financed them out of their own profits. And such conceptions apparently stuck in the minds for a while, as is shown particularly in the heavy propaganda struggle against the conclusion as to "profitability" of an industrial branch or the extent of its realized profit to justify expansion. Likewise the relative independence in the use of own means, at least in the early years of the "planning period" because of existing inadequate development of planning and control methods, may have continued.

With the progressive development of the planning system, this independence was undoubtedly restricted considerably, as the above described procedure in working out and confirming investment projects developed. The tendency toward further centralization appears to continue. Likewise a certain restricting of own means in favor of withdrawing profits, compared with the prewar period, appears to have taken place.

However, a somewhat further decline may be assumed in the exercise of influence by enterprises relative to participation with own means. Thus Dobb writes:[108] "But the distinction . . . between reinvested profits, passing through the State budget, and those which do not do so . . . apparently retains some significance for practically an enterprise or industrial branch will be able to exercise a greater influence over the use of means existing in its own name than in the use of additions granted it from above . . ." This gradation of influence runs parallel with the closer contact that naturally exists with certain enterprises participating in investing "own means," in contrast with entirely new construction, as well as with the degree of importance ascribed by the central authority to various projects; for the projects most important economically are said to be financed by the State budget to make them independent of plan fulfillment by existing enterprises.

Finally, areas are reserved for enterprises in the planning system where they can make relatively independent investment decisions. First as such are the so-called noncentralized investments. Up to 1950, smaller industrial building projects could be carried out, in addition to all kinds of outlays for communal structures, under this heading. To be sure, they were strictly limited: for "expenditures for repairs and smaller building projects, including replacement and renewal of mechanical equipment," for example, the maximum amount per project was 5,000 rubles; an essentially higher limit—100,000 rubles or the amount of insurance indemnification—is allowed only for damages caused by disasters. As source of finance for these projects certain earmarked special revenues, as for example insurance payments, the above-mentioned "own means," especially "proceed from selected portions of resources" and "mobilization of internal plant reserves" were considered. Here, therefore, own means attained significance for an enterprise, even though within very narrow limits, as previously stated.[109]

Since 1950 these decentralized investments have no longer been permitted.[110] The only remnant in this area was the right of regional organs of government, depending on their status in the hierarchy, to spend 50,000 to 100,000 rubles per project beyond the certified investment plans for equipping such local industrial undertakings as those producing building materials, fuel, or other mass products from local raw materials; financial sources are surplus revenues or lower cost expenditures of the particular public budgets as profits of the local industry which, under certain conditions, accrue more extensively to territorial corporate bodies.[111]

In addition, there was the possibility of receiving credits from *Gosbank* for "small mechanization" under the condition that they could be repaid within one year, out of the realized savings. The relevant provisions were severely criticized at the industrial conference of May, 1955, as bureaucratic and hence unworkable.[112] Yet, in August, 1955, a considerable expansion of these possibilities followed. The term of credits was extended to two years, and for some branches of heavy industry, to three years; they may now amount to one million rubles, and for large undertakings up to two million rubles. The plans may be approved by the directors themselves.[113]

Investments financed with own funds are the most important case of relatively independent investment decisions of enterprises. According to regulations still pertaining in 1951, 50 per cent of the directors' fund and 70 per cent of the staple commodity fund for investments were provided to complete, improve, and expand the production apparatus.[114] To be sure, the projects required the approval of the chief administration, while the bank that managed the means was to exercise formal control over the administration of the expenditures.[115] These rights apparently were also strictly curtailed in the early fifties, and again expanded in connection with the previously mentioned leniencies.[116]

Easing up of the principles of centralized investment planning presented thus far depends primarily on the will of the legislator. Indications of an exercise of influence by enterprises beyond this were found only in their participation in drawing up the plan and in increasing the strength of their position by handling reinvestment of depreciation charges made by an enterprise, and the State sharing of profits as "own means" of such an enterprise. However, it must now be pointed out that this system desired by the legislator is not fully adhered to. Thus complaint is heard that enterprises and other economic organizations, as well as the higher economic bureaucracy, do not adhere to the decisions as to the confirmation of investment projects. At times projects are included in investment plans and title lists the technical documentation of which is not yet available (a project task with provisional cost calculations, technical projects with main cost estimates, working plans), or inadmissible excessive costs are contained in certified cost estimates.[117] Furthermore, there was complaint as to the abuse of limit-free (*limit freie*) investments. "Frequently economic organs carry out large building projects under the pretext that it is a matter of decentralized expenditures (*limit freie*), whereby they deplete working capital, use up scarce materials, and withdraw labor strength from focal points. The estimates for decentralized expenditures need therefore to be examined carefully, especially to see whether they conform with the relevant conditions." [118] The possibility of appropriating parts of profits intended to be used according to plan has here made abuse easy and, in particular, this explains discontinuance of the condition described above.

Another starting point for abuses is the means made available by depreciation charges for major repairs, whether for current repairs, and thus to improve the short-term cost position of the enterprise, or for major repairs, and so release something from these means for expenditures that actually represent investments. To make such manipulations more difficult, banks are inserted as control agencies of expenditures of means intended for major repairs. In this way one seeks to make this control more effective in more important cases (major repairs exceeding 100,000 rubles), by transferring it from *Gosbank* to *Prombank,* specializing in investment control.[119] Finally, it must be pointed out here that even the unauthorized sale or exchange of plant parts by enterprises had become so extensive before World War II that it became necessary to take measures against it in a special regulation.[120]

At this point a word needs still to be said as to the position of planning divisions of the ministries as well as of projecting organizations. Activities and spheres of influence of these two types of organization cannot be clearly separated. We need to distinguish objectively between (1) setting investment goals, determining general principles, according to which realization of these goals is to be undertaken and projects are to be worked out, and (2) formulating individual projects, determining the specific dimensions of their components, based on these given goals and principles. This latter function we may consider the actual work of projection organizations. In some respects this is a purely routine job, particularly by connecting it with price and norm handbooks in which items of material expenditure for components of projects and their costs are standardized as far as possible. More recently there is a tendency to strengthen this connection by the transition from establishing the components to predetermining the dimensions of certain partial complexes (*Teilkomplexen*), thus to a kind of normal calculation.[121] But it is clear that such relations are not all-inclusive. Essentially the same holds for projecting organizations, as we said above, relating to the participation of enterprises in investment planning, only that here the direction is not determinable in the same manner as where occurring deviations and independent decisions operate.

The position of the planning divisions of the ministries must be considered freer. Their participation in determining of goal was discussed at the beginning of this section. Likewise, they take a prominent part in working out norm and price handbooks, and hence in fixing norms and prices. How far independence goes here we can pursue closer with the aid of a question as to the treatment of the problem of interest in investment planning. What principles are to be applied here are obviously determined independently in practice by the ministry or, for large ministries, by a chief administration. Accordingly we find here a differentiation of the principles applied according to ministries, or under certain circumstances according to chief administration. Concerning this Baumgol'c reports, incidental to a discussion of these principles and with the aid of a hypothetical illustration:[122]

> Another illustration: The transmission of energy by trans-
> mitters can be compared with transportation of fuel by rail.
> The electric works can be erected in the city and coal trans-
> ported there from a distant coal mine, or it can be erected
> at the coal mine, and energy be carried to the city by
> transmitters. For rail transport investments are larger, but
> operating costs less than for transport by transmitters. In
> comparing the variables, the ratio of savings in operating

costs to additional investment outlay in our illustration amounts to 7%. If this question is assigned to the Ministry of Transportation for a decision, the transmitter means will be built, for in the planning organization of this Ministry, a norm of 8-12% as coefficient of effectiveness is the criterion. But, if the Ministry of Power Plants[123] decides the question, the variant of rail construction[124] is recognized as most effective, since the norms in this top administration are fixed between 4-6.6%. (Norms of 4-6.6%[125] are the equivalent of pay-out periods of 15 to 25 years.[126] That is, if the additional investment funds to provide rail transport facilities, rather than transmitters, would be repaid by the savings in operating costs in 15 to 25 years or less, the Ministry of Power Plants would decide to make the rail transport investment rather than build the transmitter power lines. The pay-out period is the reciprocal of the coefficient of capital investment effectiveness expressed as a percentage.) Finally if the question is to be decided according to the norms of the planning division of the heating-power works in the Ministry of Power Works (*Teplo-elektroproekt MES*)[127] the rail construction variant is to be chosen, especially since in this largest planning organization of the Soviet Union the principle of minimizing operating costs pertains, i.e., the coefficient of capital investment effectiveness norm which is used is zero.

According to what has been said, the most widely used method[128] is planning according to the principle of minimum operating costs, without consideration of the distribution of expenditures in point of time, which alone, moreover, corresponds with official doctrine. However, the cited illustrations show that the planning organizations are actually neither bound by this general doctrine nor by instructions. This freedom finds distinct expression, especially, in the fact that an official from the area of planning railway construction authorized a *practical experiment** with respect to some previously unstudied and untried specific variant of capital investment. This experiment yielded results different from those yielded by the established method of calculation of the coefficient of capital investment effectiveness.[129]

All these illustrations show a certain easing up of the influence of the central authority on investment planning, and possibilities of independent exercise of authority in this field by lower agencies. In this connection, however, financial success viewpoints in determining their own goals must play an important role for enterprises and far-reaching also for chief administrations. These work toward rationalizing available projects by developing added capacity; it is here a question of balancing parts of projects,[130] i.e., removing "bottlenecks" within a factory, as well as realizing such smaller projects that in their complexity can be recognized and judged only by lower agencies. Above all, it is a question of rationalizing certain elements of the finishing process, and developing smaller, local raw material sources of supplies. On the other hand, it must be a question of satisfying some kind of wants not covered by the plan or that have failed because of deviation from the plan, but nevertheless remain financially effective. Here it is primarily a question of producing certain production means that remain particularly scarce; however, enterprises will rarely have unplanned production possibilities in this respect. The main instance of this is probably supplementary production of consumer goods.

Such measures in many respects represent supplementing the activity of central agencies in areas where central

* Italics supplied by editor of translation.

agencies themselves are not operating, but can merely appeal to the initiative of their subordinate agencies. This is particularly true of the decentralized rationalization of production processes. At times this is encouraged directly by central agencies, with the aid of financial stimuli, namely by providing price and rate differences that make the favored projects appear financially advantageous. As capital-intensifying objectives, reference may be made particularly to the encouragement of the development of local raw material supplies, to which reference will be made in the following chapter. However, in promoting decentralized investments, attention focuses particularly on *consumer goods** production, as indicated by the instructions pertaining to the staple commodity fund, but also by the mentioned special authorities of local and regional managerial bodies.

Insofar as these measures of the lower agencies are drawn into the regular planning system, i.e., especially insofar as a balanced type of equilibrium follows from the supplementary input and output quantities, combined with the other planned items—and that is, as said above, entirely the case with legal decentralized expenditures—it signified not only no interference with the system but rather an improvement, a possibility of closer approach to the optimal formation of the economic process. At the same time this may be the beginning of a systematically justifiable combination of material balancing and financial consistency in the planning system. Influencing planning activities of the higher economic bureaucracy, with the aid of financial means of guiding, works in the same direction. The attempts to influence the extent of consumption and production with the aid of prices and rate schedules, which are to be presented in the following chapter, are in part intelligible

* Italics provided by editor of translation.

only if one also considers the higher bureaucracy as possible addressees of these guiding measures.

By exceeding this limit, on the other hand, any loosening of the connections must lead to impairment of the plans. Thus the complaint is heard, as we noted, that there is misuse in expenditure of financial means, i.e., change in the scope of economic efforts devoted to individual purposes. In addition, there is also the disruption of the material system of coordination: investment contrary to plan, with material requirement not brought into balanced equilibrium, and the materials thus used lacking somewhere else. Insofar as the limits set on legal independence of action by enterprises merely depend on the financial regulation— and that is certainly the case with "expenditures for minor mechanization," and ultimately also with the smaller projects financed with own funds—one might even speak of a legally sanctioned gap in the material-planning system.

The importance of all these weaknesses in the material-planning system should not be overrated. Especially in investment planning, basic decisions throughout rest in the hands of the central authority. The extent of unrestricted investments, for example, during the second five year plan, amounted to four billion rubles in round number, that is to only 7 per cent of the total volume of investment.[131] But basically we see here the same duality of the guidance system that we observed in the area of general production guidance.

-–⊰ 4 ⊱–-

Principles of Price Planning

Elements of Price and Bases for Their Determination

WE WILL next consider the Soviet price system, the discussion being based on the preceding considerations and statements. To begin with, the question will be raised as to what follows solely from the development and control function for the measurement and composition of prices, from which, as shown, financial planning methods enter the Soviet guidance system. This does not require definite coefficients of choice within the price system, aside from the unavoidable guiding effect of financial performance measures intended solely for control, as indicated in the second chapter. If this guiding effect is ignored no principle can be recognized, suggesting a definite manner of weighing individual material items and classifying them in terms of this measure. Weighing is thus carried out in an arbitrary manner. From this view, it is first of all significant that two price systems have developed side by side in the Soviet Union, both of which served as controls and, in retrospect, were initially developed from novel points of view. This pertains to the two systems of *current prices** (wholesale and retail) and *constant 1926-27 prices.** The former represented the system for computing actual current turnover; the latter, on the other hand, represented only statistical prices, which were not being paid but were used to estimate material items in statistical reports of production. Since exercise of effective control and evaluation of performance of an enterprise in the first instance was based on reports of actual accomplishment submitted to the higher authority in terms of 1926-27 prices, this second price system (constant 1926-27 prices) was more effectual in many economic spheres.

Insofar as the control function of money does not merely depend on its characteristics as a measuring device, but also as means of indirectly determining performance by the buyer, money therefore becomes a quasi-medium of exchange in the formation of the price system. For therewith at least the establishing (*Herstellung*) of an additional aggregative financial relationship, as it were, is required. The receipt of money is evidence that demanded goods have been produced and distributed, and no source of money receipts may be available to producers other than from the sale of goods produced by them or entrusted to them to sell; nothing must be compensated for in the price of a good except the sum of the control values embodied in its output, i.e., the sum of prices of the input items (costs).

Conversely, the financial coverage of every outlay must be clear. As applied to the final purposes of the economy, this means that a financial relation must be established be-

* Italics supplied by editor of translation.

tween compensation for work, that achieves its set objective and the locus of price payments ultimately accruing for primary production achievement. This takes place automatically, insofar as primary producers are also intended to be recipients of the ultimate results of their performance; i.e., price payments in this case become income payments. But if a part of output is diverted to other purposes, such as, for instance, capital accumulation, this must be accomplished by withdrawing corresponding amounts from the price payments. This deduction may take place (1) when paying the initial price for productive performance, as "income tax," or (2) by paying the initial income recipients only their proportionate part of the end product, or (3) by paying out for intermediate products only a part of proceeds derived from the final product. In both (2) and (3) this may be done by a "consumption or turnover tax." At all events, price payments are apportioned among those rendering initial productive services as "net income," and the share allotted for other purposes as "tax."

"Constant prices of 1926-27" did not meet this requirement. Since they did not pertain to actual calculation of turnover, they could not be used to express the above aggregate relationships, but they could be developed further to express purely comparative statistical viewpoints. The predominant view was that of time sequence comparisons, showing the development of production in the course of years. This explains why these prices could not be used in measuring aggregate prices in the sense indicated above. Productivity is in motion, it necessarily develops differently for separate final and intermediary products, and every step in this direction must magnify the disparity between rigid (1926-27) price relationships and newly created cost conditions.

Moreover, the supposedly "constant 1926-27 prices" were by no means rigid. They were subject to changes: not as reflecting cost changes, if we may believe Western critics, notably Naum Jasny, but for totally different, primarily propaganda purposes.[1] This widened the breach (between the two systems of prices) still further.

The damages that a distorted price system can cause first became apparent with constant "prices of 1926-27." In particular, emphasis was placed on their lack of relationship to costs. Thus, there are complaints about relating production to financial growth statistics (stated in 1926-27 prices), rather than to planned material tasks. These complaints pertain not only to the calculation of the profit of a concern, but also to statistical reports of realized gross output,[2] as calculated "in 1926-27 prices." [3] Toward the end of the thirties the 1926-27 prices lost more and more of their significance, and apparently were finally abolished in 1949.[4]

Our actual interest centers in the other price system, roughly called current prices, because of its use for the actual development and computation of goods turnover between enterprises in its relationship to costs. Only this system is suited to express the cumulative aggregate relationships of the financial system. From what has been previously said, the division between cost and tax pertains to the composition of price in this system at every stage. Costs represent the sum of the financial control value of all input items in the production of a good, and again are broken down for the recipient of these value payments into taxes and costs, and ultimately into taxes and personal income (wages and salaries). Basic to price formation, naturally, are planned costs; actual costs deviate upward or downward from these, depending on the degree of successful operation of an enterprise. Hence planned costs are subdivided into actual prime costs and unplanned profit or loss. The portion of price that is a tax is subdivided into turnover tax and planned profit.[5]

Instead of a planned profit there may also be a planned loss, to be covered by a subsidy. Hence the following composition of price results:

Planned costs; operating costs
    Changes in these may result in unplanned profit or loss.
Turnover tax
Planned profit
    Instead, possibly planned subsidies.

The resultant price is called the "wholesale price of the industry," in contrast with the "wholesale price of the enterprise." The latter includes planned costs and planned profits, but no turnover tax. The retail price of consumers' goods is obtained by adding to wholesale price of the industry trade mark-up, to cover marketing and transportation costs, and possibly certain supplementary retail turnover taxes.[6] Detailed planned costs are ascertained by multiplying quantitatively fixed material input norms (see Chap. 1, p. 33) by the relevant material prices and wage rates, to which possible subsidies for various overhead costs may be added.[7] Generally, in setting prices, the procedure is the same for every industrial branch or at least for every district. Average costs of the industrial branch or group of enterprises comprising an industry are the basis of price. Of course costs differ between enterprises, whereas the wholesale selling price is the same for the products of all enterprises within an industry. This is accomplished either by (1) having the low-cost enterprises in an industry cover the deficits of high-cost enterprises, by placing a levy on the realized profits of the low-cost enterprises or on unit of product,[8] or (2) having the top administration of the industry introduce differential "accounting prices" for individual enterprises to correspond with their differential cost levels. Thus a uniform price pertains only for the customers buying from top management.[9]

An inquiry into the origin of cost relations, aside from the part played by taxes (turnover tax and planned profit) leads to a consideration of formation of prices of *primary factors of production.** With minor exceptions, *ground rent*[10] is not considered a cost factor in Russia,[11] and *interest** is considered a cost only so far as the charge for short-term bank credit is concerned; there is no cost charge for interest on total invested capital. The height of the interest rate on short-term credit is, of course, not determined by cost considerations, but merely serves for purposes of control. The amount of working capital that an enterprise is permitted to have is not based on a comparison of the disadvantages of a scarcer inventory and less liquidity, with interest costs or an improvement of these positions; but normal production periods and normal material requirements are established for separate production and material categories, and from these the relevant planned supplies needed for the planned production tasks and the requisite working capital for their financing are computed, but the computation is based on the principle of minimum cost, without regard to distribution of expenditure over time. As a rule, no interest is computed for planned long-term investment. Some planning organizations, to be sure, employ supplementary criteria analogous to interest in their investment planning, or otherwise consider varying capital intensity of individual projects.[12] In deciding upon the allotment of long-term investment funds to various uses, the preferential treatment

* Italics provided by editor of translation.

presented in the following section is operative. It leads to a differentiation of rates according to developmental needs, in that the construction of projects in underdeveloped territories is favored particularly with lower rates. This has the paradoxical effect that these rates result in making certain investments in areas that would be justified only with particularly intensive use in densely settled, already developed, and industrialized areas. On the other hand, the adoption of certain guiding effects is noticeable in the tendency to stimulate the development of a type of projects (such as exploitation of local energy reserves) by raising the interest rate applied to computing a certain alternative type of investment projects (such as centralized power plants).[13] However, a differentiation according to scarcity of means is indicated in the primitive sense that the thought of applying such criteria occurs primarily in industrial branches of the economy, where the set goals and opportunities to use the means are far more extensive than the available investment sums. Nevertheless, it is here merely a question of employment measurements for comparison of "alternatives," i.e., various alternative ways of executing projects to attain a given production goal. But they do not enter the calculation of estimated planned costs and hence do not affect prices of produced goods.

Thus only the question as to the principles governing the setting of wages remain—in particular the relative development of differential wages.[14] Initial data as to wage-setting are (1) the relations of wage gradations into which all types of labor in an industrial branch are divided,[15] and (2) the wage fund, allotted to each industrial branch and suballocated to each enterprise. The wage rate is established by dividing the allotted wage fund by the planned input units of labor, weighted according to its relative importance at all stages.[16] The classification of individual types of labor into wage categories thus naturally becomes rather standardized. And in distributing the wage fund among and within industrial branches to enterprises there is also a tendency toward further rational development of wage differentials. This rests on the fact that, in spite of all attempts with the aid of the law, to guide labor power into the desired planned direction, it has been impossible to neglect the self-interest of the worker.[17] This, however, has benefited those labor forces most that were most urgently needed to attain the set production goals. Wage relations thus have had to shift, so that occupational groups and skills that were scarcest in relation to the over-all set production goals advanced most in the evaluation. Hence, in contrast with the initially prevailing tendency toward wage equalization, their differentiation according to degree of importance of and qualification for the work has been accentuated in order to create an incentive to qualify, but primarily to do justice to the existing lack of qualified labor and to remove the inducement to exploit their situation illegally. Relative to determining the wage fund or average wage in individual industrial branches, Bettelheim mentions,[18] in addition to labor productivity (?), occupational requirements, labor qualifications, established preferences of workers for certain kinds of work, and the special needs for labor, owing to the planned growth of certain industrial branches, as factors necessitating wage inducements to attract corresponding labor forces. This corresponds with actual wage development: "The trend of change among industries was such as to raise most sharply the earnings of workers in heavy industries, while those producing consumer goods found their wages lagging behind, as a reflection of the lower importance attached to them. . . . By the mid-1930's, . . . the important wage advantage of heavy industry over light industry must have given the former a substantial edge in the competition for workers." [19]

In addition to those discussed above, the other price component is divided into turnover tax and planned profit. This twofold division is not intended to separate the share of these items left with the enterprise to be used for premiums to labor and management, to promote social welfare activities of the enterprise, and to make certain investments in the enterprise, from the share withdrawn by the State. Rather, a part of the planned profit, and regularly the largest part, is also claimed by the State for its purposes, in one form or another, by collecting it either directly in the form of a profits tax or assigning it to the enterprise for a definitely ordered investment purpose.[20] The question may be asked as to why the State's share is again subdivided into planned profit and a turnover tax and according to what principles the relative amount of each is determined. The main reason given for the State's share being in dual form is that thereby the State budget is assured of a *fixed income** from adherence to plans by the industry.[21] This reasoning, however, appears to be purely technical. Indeed, Baykov adds: "Moreover, the discrepancy between the wholesale-transfer and the cost prices of many goods is so great that the abolition of the turnover tax would result in large profits to enterprises and would weaken the inducement to observe any proper business accounting (*khozraschet*) and to run the enterprise economically." [22] Here one enters the realm of psychology. In fact, profit prescribed in the plan and collected by the State differs neither economically nor technically from a turnover tax. It is merely the expression "profit" versus "tax" that in one case gives the appearance

* Italics supplied by editor of translation.

of a realized—or not realized—free surplus, and in the other case a costlike levy, necessarily placed on the product. The actual economic significance, hidden in the above argument, will become clear in the course of the discussion.[23] Sučkov[24] gives three further reasons for the differentiation (of planned profit and turnover tax): (1) Collecting the turnover tax piecemeal makes possible the quicker transfer of extracted funds from the enterprise to the State budget; this is purely a matter of technique. (2) The supplementary control of plan fulfillment exercised by financial agencies, incidental to collecting the turnover tax. As indicated earlier, this reason is insignificant. (3) The possibility of using the turnover tax to regulate profitability. That is certainly fallacious reasoning, for planned profit, which is regulated by changes in the turnover tax rates, is again largely State income, and hence has no functional significance. Nevertheless, the third suggestion is interesting in view of the following discussion.

Nothing is said in Soviet literature as to how the height of planned profit and turnover tax, and hence of prices, is determined in its relationship to costs. For example, in the cited work by Sučkov[26] a single sentence relates to this subject: "Turnover tax rates are set by the Council of Ministers of the USSR or with its approval by the Ministry of Finance of the USSR in agreement with the interested parties." [27] However, one thing can be established, which is also implied in the reason cited above for separating the turnover tax from planned profit: the turnover tax is the actual instrument for raising means to meet the needs of the State. Accordingly it imposes very high rates on all consumers' goods,[28] while producers' goods have preponderatingly been taxed only nominally, and since 1949 have been entirely tax free.[29] Thus in 1939 the ministries of the food supply industries, textiles, and light industry,[30] as well as procurement agencies (compulsory deliveries from agriculture and the like), which represented approximately 37 per cent of the total production,[31] raised 87 per cent of the total turnover tax income of the government; the crude oil industry, with 3.1 per cent of total production, raised 8 per cent of the total, and all others, predominatingly ministries of heavy industry, representing roughly 80 per cent of total production, raised 5 per cent of the total.[32]

For planned profit no corresponding principle is conceivable that requires definite over-all apportionment among sectors of the economy. Its distribution, insofar as efforts are apparent to achieve the stimulating effect, does not pertain to total planned profit but only to those parts remaining with the enterprise. An enterprise's shares in its profits are variously graduated, according to the extent and conditions of their retention by the enterprise. Planned profit is differentiated according to:

1. Withdrawals in the form of special funds, such as Directors' Fund and Welfare Fund.
2. Profit withdrawals for the State budget.
3. Supplements to own working capital.
4. Contributions to own investment.

Only withdrawals in favor of special funds represent profit-sharing in the actual sense. Although the use of these means is also legally regulated, such uses are permitted in which the enterprise has self-interest, particularly in that part of the Directors' Fund used for premiums. Moreover, there is a definite relationship between performance of the enterprise—fulfillment or overfulfillment of profit plans— and benefits for itself in the allocation of these special funds, since special rates of planned and unplanned profits are established. The rates of participation are graduated, according to industrial branches.

> The height of payments to the Directors' Fund for enterprises of different Ministries is determined by the thought of providing an incentive to increase profit, by the characteristics of individual industrial branches, as well as by the significance of their production. For enterprises of the first group (heavy industry as well as textile industry) the withdrawals amount to 2 per cent of planned and 30 per cent of unplanned profit (i.e., savings due to lowering costs). For enterprises of the second group (primarily provision, light and local industry), the corresponding rates are 1 per cent and 15 per cent. For enterprises of some industrial branches (coal and crude oil industries, among others) as well as for all the Ministries of the smelting industry, the allocations may be higher, in exceptional cases as high as 5 per cent of planned profit and 45 per cent of unplanned profit (i.e., savings due to lowering costs). Total annual allocations to the Directors' Fund may not exceed 5 per cent of the aggregate wages of the personnel employed directly in the producing industry, based on the actual volume of commodity output.[33]

This differentiation in rates of participation and the further limitation according to the total wage quota, as well as the stipulaton that sharing by profitless-subsidized enterprises is to be computed from planned and actual cost reductions,[34] indicates clearly that the sharing of planned profits, as such, is not based on ideas of preferential treatment; in particular the rates of from 5 per cent to 45 per cent pertain to industrial branches with very low profitability; thus, in this sense, they represent equalization of an unwanted disadvantage.[35] A correspondence in this sense exists only in the use of "profit from sale of articles of mass consumption, made out of waste materials," which accrues entirely to the Welfare Fund.[36] However, this pertains to shares not related to the chief task of an enterprise, and can have only secondary significance in aggregate turnover.

The remainder of profits, embracing from 95 per cent to 99 per cent of planned profit and from 55 per cent to 85 per cent of unplanned profit, is distributed among the other three items according to the following principles: at least 10 per cent is paid to the State budget for financial control of fulfillment of the profits plan. Disposal of the remaining profit depends on the relationship between its amount and the supplementary need for working capital of the enterprise and the enterprise's investment needs. The supplemental need for working capital, in turn, is based on the relationship between planned requirements, calculated according to normal supplies of individual circulating items per unit of product and annual production tasks relative to available supplies. The need for investment means is based on the investment plans of the State. Insofar as the other sources of supply within the enterprise—the relevant parts of depreciation, as well as the mobilization of internal reserves and savings on building costs,[37]—for working capital, primarily the increase in outstanding debits,[38] and for investment, are inadequate, these needs are covered out of still remaining profit. Residual amounts are likewise paid into the State budget, and a remaining need for a subsidy is covered by allocations from the State budget. Thus, an enterprise's own profit is first used to augment working capital, so that allocations from the State budget—with rare exceptions—generally are for the purpose of financing long-term investments.[39]

As stated above, the reason given for this division of

profit[40] is the stronger incentive it gives to the enterprise to fulfill its production and profit plans, growing out of the fact that its own labor potentialities are made dependent on their equipment with working capital and on their own plant development. This type of argument, which is typical of Russian discussion of economic problems under the heading "stimulation," should not mislead us to consider the corresponding shares of profit as actually "own means" of the enterprise. Such discussion pertains primarily to the supplementary working capital, which actually gives an extended freedom of action to the enterprise, "maneuverability," and requires the least specific accounting as to its use. But generally it represents only a minor part of profit. On the other hand, as previously indicated, contributions to own investment are treated almost the same as the means obtained from the State budget, insofar as control of their source and expenditure is concerned; they must be turned over to *Prombank*, may even be forcibly requisitioned, are released only on the basis of the same accounting procedure as are budgetary means, and any greater influence the enterprise exercises over their expenditure is conjectural. Again, the difference is more psychological than functional, and in itself is insufficient to warrant differentiating between planned profit and turnover tax.

Furthermore, there is no relationship between the extent of required means for meeting planned goals, and the height of planned profits. Regulating the division of profit indicates that these two magnitudes originate independently of each other, and hence have to be taken into account subsequently. Nor can such a relationship be established for each separate enterprise. Even working capital requirements will be allocated unequally among enterprises of an industrial branch, and the need for investment must be concentrated intermittently at a few places. But selling price must be the same for all producers in an industry, and to connect progressive development of production with the allocation of cost differences would be meaningless since, in the socialist economy, selection of management of a plant proceeds from different viewpoints.

Moreover, there is no such relationship between the height of planned profits and requisite means—output intentions —for separate industrial branches as such. Concerning this Batyrev and Sitnin complain: "Fixing of profits according to plan in individual industrial branches and enterprises does not yet proceed fully according to these objectives," namely, stimulating production, graduated as to its importance. "Thus, for example, in some branches of heavy industry and of machine construction (coal mine construction, factories for heavy machine construction, etc.) planned profit is very low. Enterprises in these industrial branches turn primarily to the State budget to finance fulfillment of their investment plans and to increase their working capital, which does not create for them the requisite interest in fulfilling cost- and accumulation plans. . . . Conversely, excessive profitability of some branches of the food- and light industry, with a relatively slow rate of growth of their investments and of increases in their working capital, necessitates transferring a part of their accumulations from profit to turnover tax, since the profits of these enterprises exceed their necessary use of means for expanded reproduction so far, that their incentive to strive for lower prime costs and increased accumulation is weakened." [41]

These conditions in the distribution of profits still exist today, in that budgetary allotments to heavy industries vastly

exceed their payment of profit, while consumer goods industries pay far more in profits than the allotments they receive
from the State budget.

Moreover, apportionment of profit, as suggested in the
above quotation, would naturally not be economically rational. Raising capital is not a question of price formation
but of use of income; in this connection, therefore, it is a
matter of taxation. Hence it should be financed out of the
general budgetary funds, which should be raised by taxes
not affecting cost prices, and not be based on the calculation
of a particular planned profit. In addition to turnover tax to
raise the requisite budgetary means, planned profit has
meaning only as a uniform small mark-up of total costs for
all industrial branches, and possibly also for enterprises (including turnover tax) to ease its financial position, in case of
minor cost fluctuations, and at the same time to form the
basis for sharing interest of the personnel of the enterprise.

Such a uniform establishing of planned profit has lately
been suggested. "Wholesale prices are fixed at a level which
assures concerns an average profit of 4 to 5 per cent on commercial prime costs. . . . As is known, prices of means of
production, as a rule, are planned at the height of average
prime costs plus 4 to 5 per cent." [42] But available factual
data to date (1957) cannot be reconciled with this assertion,
nor can the tendencies presented subsequently, relevant to
price regulation from certain viewpoints. Thus it apparently
pertains only to a suggested policy statement that may perhaps have significance as an indication of certain trends of
thought developing in the economic bureaucracy, but certainly is not significant for the analysis of the existing price
system.

Thus far we were able to establish the principles of turnover tax measurement inadequately, since there are many

detailed allocation possibilities for the indicated fiscal purpose, and how the height of planned profit is determined
has likewise remained unanswered. The next question to
be considered is in how far these two components of price,
and in particular the turnover tax, figure in the regulation
of individual prices. But before we can examine this question, we must determine the point of view from which
prices in general are regulated in the Soviet Union, and
what effects such regulation wants to achieve.

Viewpoints of Price Regulation

Statements made regularly with almost stereotyped repe-
tion as principles of price formation are totally meaningless:

> The Soviet State sets prices on the basis of the commodity
> value (costs) . . . even though the prices are established by
> us on the basis of value, that does not necessarily mean that
> prices for all commodities equal their value. Based on its
> interests in developing the Socialist economy, the Soviet
> State at times makes it necessary to permit planned devia-
> tion of price from value. . . . In every case, the deviation
> of prices from value with us in the USSR proceeds according
> to plan, determined by general public interests. But value
> remains the basis of price; the sum of prices of produced
> goods is equal to their total value, and this basic element
> of price usually is expressed in the structure of the price of
> the individual product.[43]

As is at once apparent, these "principles" tell us nothing
more than that prime costs of production are to be considered somewhere in price formation, but allow any desired
margin for manipulation in determining costs, as well as in
fixing the relation of costs and price in individual cases, and

give no further basis for determining them than the "general public interests." This does not suggest trying to derive principles of price formation, which are practically applicable, but merely indicates the effort to justify a given, unexplained price system in terms of Marxian value dogma.

Attempts to discover practically applicable, meaningful principles of price formation are rarely found. Only questions that have significance for the large circle of lower economic managers and for other personnel entrusted with managerial functions are treated systematically in textbooks. These deal almost exclusively with techniques of plan execution. On the other hand, the higher authorities of the economic bureaucracy who handle price formation do not want to be restricted in their freedom of action, by general principles. This finds theoretical expression in the discussion of the relationship between economic legality and planning under socialism. Many variations appear in the manner in which the nature and meaning of economic legality under socialism is determined. In general, there is the recurring tendency to emphasize exclusively the creative power and automatic excellence of the plan, and by means of hazy reservations to clear away all necessary connections with economic principles.[45] As indicated in the second chapter, no particular role is assigned to the "law of value," and hence to prices as "regulator of production."

But attempts to develop a theoretically closed system of price formation principles, incomplete as they may be, cannot be overlooked. As evidence I should like to cite a work by Tureckij, which was reviewed by Arakeljan and Mstislavskij.[46] The review reproduces his thought as follows: "In the book by Prof. Tureckij a certain 'price system' evolves, in which the final criterion for the planned fixing of the price of every individual commodity is the needs for profitability of the industrial branches producing the commodities, and the attainment of maximum satisfaction of consumers (p. 339). The author asserts that in price planning "the solution of two problems (assurance of a fixed price level of products and a correct system of price proportions) will achieve, simultaneously, the combination of interests of producers and of consumers. . . . (p. 341). Such a price system reminds one of price formation without value, defended by vulgar bourgeois economists, where prices are the resultant of crossing of 'forces' of producers (striving to cover their costs) and of consumers (seeking to influence the most advantageous price relationships for themselves, through fluctuations in demand)." [47]

The criticism of this interpretation lies in labeling it as leaning on bourgeois theorems and in the reference to "admitted separation of price from value as stated in the book." [48] In addition, there is the rejection of the abstract one-sided disposition of the problem of price planning. "The book erroneously attributes to Soviet prices the role of sole economic criterion for planning production [pp. 341, 351, 354-355]. Naturally, Soviet prices are formed with the intention of stimulating those processes which strengthen and develop the Soviet economy. However, Soviet price cannot serve as sole economic or social economic criterion for the organization of production in enterprises, organization of transportation, and justification of investment projects. In such a one-sided conception of the economic criterion, neither historical conditions for price formation nor the specific historical problems of either this or that part of the Soviet economy are given consideration." [49]

The motives and ideas actually allowed to guide price

planning are presented only occasionally and briefly, as a rule, in articles in periodicals with semipractical objective—reference to defects appearing in practice—written by authors belonging to the economic bureaucracy or who are close to it. Thus it is naturally impossible to separate, with any degree of certainty, the views of the author and the exposition of actually applied principles. But at least this much can be said: no pervasive principle of price regulation can be established. The effective thoughts and forces not attuned to each other in a logically closed system must be assembled from pertinent occasional remarks and developed, moreover, out of certain typical regularities that become visible in the formation of prices.

This situation as to source materials, furthermore, necessitates basing the investigation on statements and facts extending over a longer period of time. Naturally a certain development has taken place during this period, and their tendencies will be indicated, as far as they can be recognized. In general, the development of planning principles takes place only very gradually in such an enormous apparatus as the Soviet Union, so that this cautiously employed procedure should be permissible. Repeated assertions as to radical changes in Soviet price policy rest on the overemphasis placed on occasional, individual remarks.

The views as to principles of price regulation in the Soviet Union may be analyzed under five headings (*Begriffe*). These are:

The budgetary viewpoint (*Optik*)
Planning technique
Preferential treatment
Consumption guidance
Production guidance[50]

The two aspects theoretically least fruitful will first be discussed briefly. The *budgetary view* is emphasized particularly by Jasny. He shows that inflation of prices of consumers' goods by means of the turnover tax (and two other factors) and the holding down of prices of the means of production by subsidies (and several other factors), together with a partial shifting of expenditures under other headings in the budgetary plan, makes the share of State expenditures in the national income and the ratio of outlays for new investments and defense to total expenditures appear much smaller than they actually are, and implies that realizing this effect has been one of the basic factors in forming the price system.[51] As will be shown later, granting of subsidies is sufficiently explained by other, more important reasons,[52] which eliminates such an argument as primary reason, or at least makes it plausible that such considerations played a secondary role.

As to the view of *planning technique,* a reference is found in the discussion of so-called "wholesale delivered prices." [53] These "assure . . . uniform prices at all places of consumption and create a stable basis for calculating prime costs of industrial production and for drawing up cost estimates for investment planning." [54] Especially for industrial construction, "the costs of the principal supplied materials, prepaid at point of delivery,* are uniform for all construction within a given district, requiring no separate calculation for every building project." [55] The view here indicated has far greater significance than appears in this meager reference. Merely to make possible technical mastery of planning and control work requires not only securing a certain uniformity of the price material on which planning rests as well as of material norms, at least for certain areas of the economy,

* Net delivered prices.

but also its permanence and stability over certain periods of time.

Uniformity of numerical data, moreover, facilitates carrying out planning and calculation proceedings in accordance with desired principles, and simplifies their control. In part, it even makes possible replacing the separate calculation of every single building project with a normal calculation, by working out a substantial number of similar or at least relatively similar projects, or those having features similar to the projects to be developed. At times, savings in costs incidental to simplification of planning work may even compensate for cost disadvantages resulting from giving up consideration of realizable opportunities for savings from separate calculation in specific cases.

A certain constancy of numerical data (prices and also norms) over periods of time is therefore necessary, since the requisite mechanism of price and norm handbooks for carrying out planning calculations, and in particular for projecting investment plans, is evidently so extensive that it cannot be kept adjusted to a more flexible price structure nor to a more flexible system of technical coefficients. Publication of appropriate price and norm handbooks before the war proceeded at nine-month intervals, and the last price reforms before the outbreak of the war did not get into the price handbooks at all. Thus work was carried on, in part, for several years with obsolete data, since for solely technical reasons it was simply impossible to make the adaptations.[56] Podsivalenko wrote regarding the consistency of the handbooks: "It is known that (in 1952) the handbooks of the extended estimate norms of 1937-1938, which form the basis for drawing up cost estimates for building construction, have not been revised since the date of their issue." [57] Finally, on January 1, 1955, new norm handbooks for building construction were introduced.[58]

The particular inelasticity appearing here was naturally connected with the confusion of the war and postwar years and the resultant overburdening of the managerial apparatus with other problems. But this alone does not explain it; there must also be more general contributing reasons. The rigidity of the economic planning apparatus may be traced primarily to the greater requirement of control, which does not permit substituting of data by free estimates, but which requires carrying out all specifications with officially recognized material; for otherwise the State, placing orders, would have to fear far more than a private enterpriser that supplementary estimates might be made, to its disadvantage, by some illegal private interest. Likewise, every change of prices or norms may create considerable difficulties in the development of long-term building projects.

In summary, it can be said that for technical planning reasons the need exists to keep prices as uniform as possible, even if the evaluated production elements are not completely similar, and not to consider fully the multiplicity of possibilities to employ these items in making calculations. It is also necessary to keep prices constant over possibly long periods of time, and therefore to neglect certain changes in production possibilities and in the relative importance of these goods.

The actual economic trends of thought relative to the question of price regulation or, in general, to the formation of financial conditions of production, may best be summarized by the concept "preferential treatment." The thought expressed above that carrying on production with financial criteria is an affair of the capitalistic market and that the actual goals of socialist economic management are deficient in this respect indicates, conversely, that the consequences of the financial planning system must be grasped, in order to justify the economic goals of a Socialist State. The simplest form of this penetration is maintenance and development of production, without considering condition of costs. In view of the otherwise prevailing aggregate financial relationship, this indicates the necessity to cover deficits out of the State budget by means of *subsidies,* when they occur. In this way the thought of preference arises from a completely negative attitude toward the functional use of the price system; it thus presents no view for price regulation, but rather implies a given price system whose disturbing effects on the material plan are removed, no matter how, by preferential financial treatment of the industrial branch to be promoted: namely, by subsidies. But the relationship between the extent of subsidies and the height of prices cannot be overlooked, and since determining the latter also rests in the hands of the State, its consideration in the choice of measures for financial preference of the industrial branch to be promoted becomes unavoidable. The transition to a functional use of the price system arises, as shown above, in spite of its rejection, out of the force of circumstances. Every refinement of financial preference will have to be combined with a regulation of the height of prices. The basic objection to the directive effect of the financial system leads not only to a certain inconsistency in the measures taken, but also to an inner contradiction in the state of confirmations.

A first price-regulating measure is contained in the shifting of subsidies from industries to be fully promoted to producers of their intermediate products. Deficits covered by the State are permitted to occur even in the production of intermediate products, thus making these available at artificially low prices to the industries to be promoted. Conversely, financial preference also appears by permitting particularly high selling prices of output, worthy of preferential treatment. The underlying thought here is that the resultant profits, used as premiums for workers and particularly for expansion of investment, make possible a more rapid development of this production.

The reason for the measures in these cases fluctuate between financial support of complete materially planned production projects and financial stimulation of such undertakings, whose execution is not made possible by the material plan. In the second case the transition is given to the regular insertion (*Einsatz*) of prices to guide production (or consumption), discussed subsequently.

This type of argument is also given in relation to the initial direct subsidies. "In the course of the first five year plan, industrialization necessitated maintaining low prices for products of heavy industry. Low prices for metal and coal meant low prices for machines, and thus created a supplementary stimulus to the introduction of machinery in all branches of the national economy."[59] In view of the fact that investments were predominantly centrally planned, it might here be a matter more of an embellished rhetorical phrase than of reproduction of an actually effective consideration. Nevertheless, even as such it reveals the change in views toward the price system.

Subsidies played a particularly important role at the beginning of the period of industrialization. Chief recipients, in the first place, were coal mining and then the steel industry; then followed various machine industries and ore mining, production of nonferrous metals and various building materials, including building lumber.[60] Actually, machine building industries were favored first: subsidies paid to the remaining industries, especially to coal mining, also served indirectly to foster these industries. Moreover, the return to subsidies, after their abolition had been express-edly proclaimed in 1936, indicates that the reasons cited above gave only a partial explanation of the "introduction" of subsidies, and that other causes, to be explained below, must have contributed to their origin. Also, the price reforms of 1949-50 pursued the avowed purpose of abolishing subsidies.[61] I cannot say in how far it succeeded. Jasny suspects the opposite.[62]

It may be said, in criticism of the pursued trend of thought, that the idea of preference rests on the misconception of the price system, as previously indicated in the second chapter. The desired objective could be attained just as well if, instead, the means used as subsidies were placed at the direct disposal at the points of use of final output, i.e., of the enterprises that are to operate the newly constructed machines and plants, especially when, as is here generally the case, the State itself is the buyer of the end products produced with the aid of subsidies, so that no disadvantage is apparent if it pays the requisite sums to cover all costs with prices, instead of in the form of sub-sidies. On the contrary, the disadvantage appearing in the case of indirect subsidies would be avoided in that other buyers of the intermediate products, who were not intended to be favored to this extent, participate in the artificially low prices of the items involved.

Nor are these relationships fully perceived if one turns away from the system of subsidization. As a rule, criticism voiced of this system relates solely to the apparent weaken-ing of *khozraschet* (understood as financial control of plan). "The system of state subsidies . . . destroys the basis for *khozraschet*—the coincidence of outlays and resultant product, the covering of expenditures with the 'own' means of the enterprise. The system of state subsidies accustoms enterprises to live at the expense of the State budget, weakens the incentive to strive to lower prime costs, and contradicts the policy of strengthening the Soviet ruble." [63] This objection pertains only if subsidization is incorrectly handled. Granting of subsidies can very well be so organized as to be connected with the method of *khozraschet*. For this purpose it is merely necessary to establish a fixed relationship between the height of the granted subsidy and the volume of output. This is done at present. In granting subsidies a "supplementary norm per unit of finished product or per ruble of output" is established, which is granted by the Ministry of Finance. Subsidized enterprises must submit periodic "operation reports" to *Gosbank*, stating quantity, value, and subsidy norm for delivered products, and on payment of subsidies, *Gosbank* has to determine whether the requisitioned sum corresponds with the granted subsidy norm. Savings of subsidies resulting from unplanned lowering of costs contribute to deductions from the saved sums in favor of the directors' fund, and likewise afford further financial allowances, even as in case of realizing unplanned profits.[64]

Aside from the previously cited reasons for the budgetary aspect and planning techniques, two other reasons can justify the system of subsidies, at least in part. On the one hand it relates to the question of price formation in those industries still in the developmental stage. Here it is very likely that developmental costs over longer periods of time, possibly for years, are higher in the long run than those anticipated, and accordingly that one is neither willing nor able to burden the buyer of this initial output with these higher costs. However, strictly speaking, it is here not a matter of subsidies, i.e., lost grants in aid, but rather a special kind of investment, also well known in Western economic systems. Costs of breaking in new concerns belong to investment costs as much as those of erecting the plants; they must likewise be reimbursed subsequently in the price when normal production is begun.

The other consideration relates to the defense economy. In view of imminent warlike disagreements it is possibly necessary to have supplementary production and transportation facilities available that cannot be fully used in peacetime and the operation of which is too costly, but which are intended to supplement productive capacity of the war economy or provide reserve capacity in case of destruction. Here consideration must be given in particular to maintaining such capacities in more protected areas or, more generally, in decentralized locations. In this case actual subsidies are justified. They are intended to cover that part of supplementary cost arising out of the less favorable location, chosen for military reasons, or out of excess capacity. In both cases it is therefore not a matter of distorting the financial value system with subsidies but one of supplementing it.

These two points of view are also expressed in Soviet literature. The connection between subsidies and development is strongly emphasized: "If heavy industry had been deprived of subsidies, while production technique still limped along and costs were high, it would have led to a pronounced increase in the price of products of heavy industry. Such a price increase would have boosted the entire economic price system." [65] In particular, comparison between short-term and long-term profitability, which was presented above, together with its consequences,[66] represents especially an emphasis on the limitations experienced by a profitability criterion, from the viewpoint of developmental difficulties of infant industries. However, as indicated above, it is not clear whether consideration of these developmental difficulties fits into the framework of a financial valuation system or "profitability system." There are also frequent references to pushing forward of territorial defense views in investment planning, where these are again simply conceived of as negation of the profitability criterion, instead of attempts to incorporate them in the financial guidance system.

The indicated views are particularly significant for the development of raw material reserves, especially of second grade coal reserves, and in general of heavy industry in the Urals and beyond; the steel works of the East, as is well known, were developed primarily with Ural ores and Kuzbass coal.

From the view of preferential treatment, we found the transition to a still rather hazy and inconsistent but nevertheless distinctive handling of prices to achieve economic guiding effects and their use as lead criteria. There are three reasons for the open injecting of this thought into planning practice. (1) As just shown, one hit upon the relationship of the height of prices and the extent of subsidies in the purely routine treatment of price setting, and so became accustomed to regulate prices, with such effects in view. (2) As indicated in detail in the second chapter, it was discovered that prices set solely for financial control revealed a feature of their own (*Eigenleben*), namely, they induced lower agencies to independent action, which disturbed the plan and made it necessary to take these effects into account in the formation of prices. This implies, as was also explained clearly in the second chapter, that quantity arrangements are more decentralized and less controllable by the central authority than are price relations; the same price pertains to a number of quantity transactions. (3) Finally, one had to realize that in many areas of decision, particularly where quantity decisions were made by a large number of lower agencies, prices were the item most accessible for central planning and control, and so concluded that certain guiding effects that could not be attained in the desired manner by the central authority with direct quantity decisions could be achieved with the aid of price manipulation.

Now prices can be used on the one hand to influence the extent to which either intermediary or end products are employed for further production or for fulfillment of ultimate purpose, i.e., to guide consumption, and on the other to influence the decision as to volume of output of individual producers, i.e., to guide production. As such, these are naturally only two aspects of the same planning and guiding process, at least insofar as it pertains to intermediate products or means of production, which forms the core of this investigation. These cannot be separated to any great extent, but in every single case are either incorporated jointly in the material planning process or subjected to financial orientation, since the producible quantity for every producer is dependent on the extent of available producers' goods. Nevertheless, the inevitability of financial guiding measures first appears in the question of consumption guidance, since the distribution in kind of the produced quantities, because of their complexity, is far more difficult to control than is the measurement of the volume of production. Accordingly, this view first attracted attention and is even now being given serious consideration.

It would appear that planning of prices of consumers' goods should have formed the starting point. Undoubtedly it is receiving a certain amount of consideration. Mention was made in the first chapter of certain references to price elasticities in planning consumer goods requirements, i.e., retail trade turnover, but, as was indicated there, the practical significance of these observations is questionable. More frequently such references are found in the more general form, in that attention is called to the consideration of supply and demand in forming prices of consumers' goods. But this attention is focused more on total supply relative to total demand, and it is typical to view price formation in "commercial trade" of the State and especially in the free *kolkhoz* markets in times of crises and war as particularly noteworthy cases for application of such views of price formation.[67] These are situations where everything depends on regulating total demand because of generally inadequate supply, while financial guidance of demand for specific goods appears futile. Thus occasional specific references[68] must be considered with reservations. In view of known surplus of purchasing power, to be considered in more detail subsequently, financial guidance of the sale of all secondhand consumers' goods would be ineffective and, in particular, stimulation of sales would be superfluous.[69] This condition, of course, changes as soon as removal of the surplus purchasing power is successful. I cannot say in how far this is currently the case. There are some indications of stabilization.

Most illustrations of financial guidance of consumption pertains to means of production, especially to raw materials and semifinished products. "The relation between prices of scarce metals and their substitutes is designed to economize in the use of the scarce materials, to combat material losses and to stimulate the wider use of substitutes." [70]

These tendencies also become clearly visible in transportation, particularly since the price reform of 1949. Its chief innovation consisted of relating basic railway freight rates to prime costs, whereas before then the railway system had operated extensively on the principle of subsidizing certain types of goods, and charging what the traffic would bear (for goods in general).[71] However, this principle is applied only with certain typical exceptions. "In the new rates the principle of differential rates for appropriate hauling distances is applied more consistently than formerly. Thus it is known that prime costs of hauling per ton kilometer decrease with increasing distances. Nevertheless the new rates do not provide lower rates for long hauls for a large number of shipped goods, but in a number of cases even allow an increase in rates for shipment over stretches exceeding normal distance." [72] * In particular, higher rates are set for very long hauls, exceeding 2,000 km. This is intended to stimulate the use of local raw materials: especially to encourage the development of heavy industry in newly developed centers, to promote diversification of plants in such an area, and thus to make these plants independent of the supply of intermediate products from old but distant centers of heavy goods production.[73]

Likewise freight rates for short hauls, below 50 km., were raised twofold to fourfold, and in addition motor truck rates were lowered in 1950, to stimulate transition to truck transportation for these distances. Furthermore, railway freight and inland water shipping rates were so correlated

* Illustration omitted, p. 154, paragraph 1, lines 16-20, of original.

as to stimulate transition to the use of waterways paralleled by railway lines. Especially for periods of the year when waterways were open, higher railway rates were established for many goods. Finally, there were special lower freight rates to encourage the use of cars otherwise empty and there are penalty rates for unused space or weight within a car, as well as for cross-shipments.[74]

In transportation the financial guidance of production becomes particularly apparent. However, in itself it is not an alternative to financial guidance of use, but supplements it by assuming a special function. This pertains to so-called "net wholesale delivered prices," which were introduced more extensively in 1949, especially for iron and lumber. They had begun to be used even before the war, relative to cement, glass, rubber, tile, and several other building materials as well as to crude oil products.[75]

Aside from its justification as a means of achieving price uniformity for technical planning reasons, previously presented, this transition appears as an adjustment measure, to adapt financial guidance of transportation to varying situations. It should be borne in mind that buyers of intermediate products and of consumers' goods who were to be induced to consider transportation costs in selecting the most favorable source of supply and the most suitable means of transportation could actually have no influence on either one, for they had to be satisfied if their demands were considered in any way or anywhere, while the shipper chose transportation means that suited his convenience; in brief, a "seller's market" existed for most products. The guidance system thus had to be so reconstructed that not the buyers but the sellers were financially interested in the choice of shipping methods and means. Hence, the appeal to financial interest no longer turned to enterprises in their capacity as recipients or buyers of goods, but rather as sellers or producers.

This is the purpose of

"... net wholesale delivered prices ... insofar as suppliers of products have to pay transportation costs directly, their interests in lowering these costs and in using shipping means rationally is increased. ... With the transition to net wholesale delivered prices, all outlays for transportation products are borne by the selling organizations and are included in the wholesale price of the industry. Insofar as shipping costs are borne directly by the selling organization of an industry, its financial results, i.e., the height of profits or losses, will depend on correct planning of the flow of goods. That means that the selling organizations are forced to explore systematically the geographic distribution of output and use of their goods, to draw up regional balances of production and consumption, to devise rational plans for shipping products from production to consumption regions, and to seek ways to shorten hauling distances and provide the cheapest transportation." [76]

With the introduction of financial guidance methods in the transportation sector, the transition to financial guidance of production appears in still another way. The alternative confronting the buyer frequently is not whether to purchase from a closer source with more favorable transportation, or to purchase from a more distant, less favorable location, but rather whether to purchase from a distant producer or develop the production of the wanted product within the enterprise itself. This alternative pertains particularly to the development of such local energy resources as coal (usually of poorer quality) and peat deposits (whether used directly for fuel or for the production of electric energy) and also to local output of building materials.[77]

Here rate policy and immediate price policy are combined. For it is intended to achieve the same goal by price-setting itself. Thus the relative prices of transported energy and locally produced energy are intended to stimulate a transition to local energy production.[78] "Other illustrations can be found of attempts to influence the choice of goods to be produced, as well as the quality and quantity of output, with the aid of price-setting. Variations in profitability of some types of production are also adopted to stimulate introduction of new product-mixes, and to assure plan fulfillment of output of goods which have particular economic significance, as for example especially important forms of rolled metal, etc." [79, 80]

Finally, it appears to be recognized that the effects of price setting on production and consumption are interrelated and normally supplement each other. "Prices are to be fixed with a view to stimulate output of particularly scarce or specially needed products, and at the same time to limit their use in production." [81] Majzenberg[82] also states that the prices of coal are set so as to manifest the simultaneous tendency to increase its output and to achieve economies in its use.

But recognition of this fact does not yet mean comprehensive development of the price system into an integrated system of values, in accordance with the principles set forth at the beginning of the second chapter. It must be borne in mind, in particular, that required (financial) guidance effects do not develop by themselves out of the relationship between prices and costs, as should be the case. Automatically, for example, the shift from rail to motortruck transportation for shorter hauls, if based on costs, should with normal rates merely indicate that the latter is cheaper in this rationally established hauling area. Where this is

not the case, even shipping distances of less than 50 km.
should use rail transportation. Instead, in the cited cases,
the guidance effects are used artificially as deviations of
prices from costs. "The Soviet State sets the prices of individual products in relation to prime costs at varying
levels, and in doing so, considers conditions of production
and demand, as well as the composition of the consumer
area and the many-sided problems of economic policy." [83]

This might be explained, in part, by the fact that not all
conditions of "scarcity" that should be considered in formulating costs of production are actually present. As previously
indicated, generally only outlay for *labor** is considered in
costs, not the use of *capital** and *land,** the latter including
natural scarcity of raw materials. That some thought is
being given to this fact in price manipulation is indicated
by the frequent reference to "scarcity of materials" to
illustrate (financial) guidance of use. . . .

In other cases, it appears to be a matter of seeking to influence decisions with financial stimuli that relate, as it
were, to the qualitative aspect of the economy. In such cases
correct adherence to the appropriate cost factor would be
difficult, even if one were not restricted as to the applicable
cost concept by the labor value dogma. This may, for example, be the reason for rate discrimination for so-called
excessively long hauls insofar as considerations of strategy
play a role.

There is a third related case. It may be that cost relationships, which in themselves express the economic significance
of the evaluated factors correctly, do not produce the desired effect because the peculiarities of costs arising later in
the production process or certain secondary effects connected with the use of this or that factor cause the lower

* Italics supplied by editor of translation.

agency doing the choosing to make an irrational decision. Consider, for example, why transition to better types of roofing must be stimulated, especially by changes in price relations. Observe that, in the choice of the cheaper grade, savings become apparent immediately upon completing a structure, while cost disadvantages show up only over the years in the form of increased cost of repairs, and the need for more rapid renewal. If we consider the pressure put on enterprises to lower costs of construction of new projects, it becomes understandable why they live a hand-to-mouth existence and accept a far greater disadvantage for later years in order to achieve a small temporary advantage during construction.[84] Likewise plant managers who are under constant pressure to fulfill the plan and who are frequently hampered by scarce or inadequate supply of materials are not inclined to ship urgently needed materials by slow waterways if they can get them more rapidly by rail, even at certain cost disadvantages.[85]

In both cases, financial guidance methods are used to achieve desired results, to stimulate, just as though there were no relationship between the dosage of guidance means and the extent of obtained result. Such handling of financial guidance is popular with Soviet planners, since, as shown in the second chapter, they found the idea of financial guidance useful to stimulate productive effort of those who carried out the plan as to stated objectives, i.e., their understanding of financial guidance primarily psychological, and only gradually they found out its economic implications. This becomes even clearer in another case: It may happen that actually prevailing cost differences should suffice to justify a real change, as, for instance, transition to another type of production or transportation, but no such change takes place because the cost difference is not big enough to jar those responsible for carrying out the plan out of their customary tempo. Since no continuing comparison takes place between the prevailing method and alternatives, conceivably gradual changes in relative costs of several methods would not induce a corresponding revision of the prevailing method of production, whereas a single greater change in relative costs, a sudden shock, would make those responsible conscious of the fact that something has changed and that a revision of prevailing methods is in order.

Insofar as such a situation exists, overdosages must be used if it is intended to achieve certain results with the aid of financial guidance methods; prices must be lowered more than costs if a suitable expansion of consumption is to be achieved; prices must rise more than costs if consumption is really to be curtailed. The planner then is like a man driving a car with jammed steering gear down a hill; alternately he has to jerk with full force to the left and to the right in order to attain a deviation from the traveled course to the pursued one, and every such jerk probably steers beyond the desired direction to the other extreme.

Such shock tactics, indeed, appear to play a considerable role in Soviet price policy. The illustrations of financial guidance of consumption, previously cited, relate to only a very small segment, but nevertheless deal consistently with the operation of large changes, ranging from 25 and 40 per cent to several times the initial prices and costs. Moreover, they are well suited to the peculiarities of the Soviet method of operation. There is a peculiar hostility to theory in Soviet thinking, an aversion to specific lines of economic thought processes, a certain inclination to solve problems simply and arbitrarily. This is revealed, for example, in the cited effort to treat the question of the relationship between performance and compensation not economically but psychologically. It also becomes apparent in the method of "pace setters," in the choice of basic developmental goals, in the principle of "complex mechanization," and in the choice of the degree of technical development of individual branches of production and of finishing processes. Everywhere there is the inclination to primitive, tangible, conspicuous goal setting, to bigness, to forceful action. All this is in sharp contrast with the careful equating analysis in our Western economic thinking, based on the idea of an equilibrium of infinitesimal marginal magnitudes.

Such a manner of thinking is typical on the one hand of the politician, especially of the demagogue and the revolutionary, who has no understanding of complex relationships but has to arouse enthusiasm for easily understandable goals, and whose thoughts, therefore, tend toward correspondingly simple concepts that emphasize primarily the importance of action and determination. On the other hand, it is also characteristic of the practical economist who constantly looks askance at the complexity and abstraction of theory and rather tends to relate his own decisions to a few quick rules of thumb. In a State whose intellectual life is obsessed with dogmatic intolerance, these habits of thought of the rulers must necessarily permeate all economic thinking. However, the so-called shock tactics are undeniably to some extent practically justifiable. Actually, economic guidance is not merely a matter of constructing a consistently coordinated value system directed toward a goal, but primarily faces the task of economic guidance of the masses. A guidance system in its over-all scope not adapted to the reactions of these masses is ineffective, no matter how well it may be balanced. It is a moot question whether the crudeness of the shock tactics rests on the incapacity of the leaders or on the peculiarity of the assigned tasks. In addition, correct coordination toward attaining a goal in a rapidly developing economy as well as setting up of developmental goals is scarcely possible anyway.[86]

The separation of prices from costs in order to achieve intended guidance effects might, therefore, also find its explanation and justification in the fact that the Soviet price system does not proceed from marginal costs but, rather, uses average costs. Actually, the appropriate directing effect of cost prices results only if prices are based on marginal costs. Only marginal costs can express adequately the usefulness of available factors of production in terms of the input of the last unit of the factor employed, and hence its over-all economic scarcity.[87] A price system based on average costs has to introduce supplementary corrective factors if it is to reflect such scarcities.

It might be assumed that the cases that involve price manipulation in practice to guide consumption in Soviet Russia also apply to production where marginal costs deviate considerably from average costs. Conscious relation of price formation to marginal costs does not pertain here either. For this would require paying certain theoretical as well as practical attention to the phenomenon of marginal costs, but marginal cost theories are discredited in Russia as "vulgar, bourgeois economy." Furthermore, measurement of corrective factors in price formation, as we saw, occurs from totally different, actually contradictory viewpoints; conscious orientation would not be limited by the number of times corrections are made, but would have to include the degree of the correction.

Nor can it be assumed that marginal cost deviations act as unconscious inducements to make corrections. On the contrary, we can observe that efforts are being made to approach the problem of varying marginal costs in another manner, where it turns up unavoidably, namely, in the higher costs of inefficiently operating concerns. It has been reported that efforts are being made to adjust such cost differences by levies or differentiated accounting prices within the trusts or top managements of the ministries. With such differentiation between whole production aggregates as, for example, between different producing areas, it often happened that industries considered most important and most worthy of promoting were secretly favored with preferential cost purchases of intermediary products, while other enterprises mutually pushed off on each other the costliest sources of supply.[88] These cost differences have considerable significance because of the different rates of development of centrally managed and local industries and because of the emphasis on exploitation of second-rate sources of raw materials, of which more presently.

We must now inquire how the idea of production guidance operates with the aid of price fixing in relating prices to costs, and the measurement of the corrective factors. The creation of a cost structure that will automatically produce the requisite guidance effect would be possible only if those who are responsible for quantity planning were, in this way, led to marginal cost reckoning and to measuring the volume of production by considering the relationship between marginal costs and prices. But the prevailing principle of financial planning is *average** cost accounting; nothing is said of deviating from it, and we must therefore assume that it is obligatory for enterprises. The enterprise thus remains obligated, even if the spread between costs and prices is enlarged to stimulate productive effort, to account for what happened to this spread, and if in expanding production it permits an increase in costs at the expense of profits, it will

---

* Italics supplied by editor of translation.

get into difficulties with fulfillment of its planned profit withdrawal and profit use plan. It is therefore induced to expand output by increased profit margins only if this is possible with proportional costs. This would be the case, particularly, if completing of one product occurred at the expense of another, i.e., with changes in the types of product. As shown in previous quotations, financial influencing of production frequently is done with an eye to influencing types of products.[89] This accords with the fact that the productive capacity of enterprises, in general, is fairly fixed, so that they cannot change their total volume of output very much.

Nevertheless we found illustrations showing efforts being made to influence by financial means those production items which can be changed only with the aid of investments. That is particularly the case where the alternative is either outside purchase of items or their production within the enterprise. Here we might perhaps assume that no tie to prescribed cost figures pertains and that therefore cost influences can be extended to the margin in determining the volume of output. To be sure, we are here dealing with influencing only one input item (other things remaining constant) while other restrictions are imposed on the enterprises (explained in "Distribution of Influence in Planning Investment" of the preceding chapter) by the control mechanism and by financing conditions.

Complete determination of disposal, based on cost and price, may finally be assumed in the production of consumers' goods made from remnants and waste materials. Here the entire profit remains with the enterprise, with the expressed stipulation to develop the relevant plant capacity. This presumably allows a relatively large freedom to the enterprise to set the price. But we are here dealing with a restricted area naturally limited by its dependence on the availability of such waste materials.

This limited effectiveness of cost and price relationships does not pertain to obligatory withdrawal of profits, insofar as the higher economic bureaucracy—ministries, top management, and their planning organizations—is the recipient of the stimuli intended to be given by price-setting. At all events, the natural financial stimuli do not affect these agencies to the same degree. In general, it is difficult to find out from available sources what viewpoints and conditions influence decisions in this area. We are limited to the observation that occasionally financial guidance measures are also applied, where scarcely anyone in this higher bureaucracy is considered a recipient. Hence a certain receptivity for such impulses must also pertain here.

Furthermore, *financial** regulation of *consumption** is also not carried out consistently in the indicated unsystematic manner but only sporadically, as are also the *material** guidance methods of regulating *consumption.** On the other hand, the use of *financial** guidance methods to regulate *production** is merely indicated as a *tendency** and *material** guidance outweighs them by far. This is due to the fundamentally negative attitude toward functional use of the price mechanism, as we have learned. It is here merely a question of examples taken from planning practice. It is naturally difficult to prove that a principle, a point of view, was not operative. Reference is first of all made here to verbal information obtained by English economists in conversations on the occasion of the Moscow Economic Conference of 1952, although naturally this is of doubtful value. Russian economists who were questioned declared that scarcity might have *no** effect on price setting.

* Italics supplied by editor of translation.

For example, binoculars were first offered for sale for 4,000 rubles and then for 3,000 rubles. But unsalable supplies accumulated at these prices. When the price was lowered to 2,000 rubles, the stocks were sold out. Nevertheless, the price was lowered further to 1,000 rubles.[90]

An example of this practice, related to means of production, is cited by Jasny, referring to price formation of timber, firewood, and building lumber. "Amazing as it may seem, the firewood price established April 1, 1936 survived the inflation not only of the following peace years but also the war and postwar years, right down to January 1, 1949. Also, the rise in the price of firewood by not quite tenfold from 1926-27 to January 1, 1949 appears quite small compared with the price increases of all other fuels, especially if one considers the great shortage of timber and the urgent necessity of curtailing the use of firewood." [91] Likewise, concerning the prices of building lumber, he observes: "They remained unchanged thereafter [i.e., after the price increases of 1936] for almost 13 years in spite of inflation, the extreme shortage of timber, and the cutting of forests far in excess of what was economically reasonable." [92, 93]

As a reason for the disproportionate technical development of industrial branches producing lime and cement, Majzenberg states: "High prime costs of lime are explained by the fact that owing to the inadequate attention paid to the lime industry by the Union Ministry for the building materials industry, and by the Council of Ministers of the Union Republics, this branch remained far behind in its technical development within the whole cement industry. At a time when the cement industry represents a highly mechanized industrial branch, the mechanization level of the lime industry is still low." [94] This difference in development is attributable to the fact that the cement industry belongs to the new industries, developed by the central authority of the Union government, while lime production as local industry is controlled by the republics and districts.[95] Apparently it was not acceptable to set the price of cement, influenced by the previously indicated idea of subsidy, as high for newly constructed enterprises whose output was intended for large, heavy industries and other urgent building projects as would have corresponded with supply conditions of related means in building construction. To do so would have exposed these urgently needed building projects to heavy cost burdens, and so have divided the economy into a preferred sector and a limping sector.

A similar phenomenon frequently occurs where, on the one hand, it is either a matter of divergent development of industry directly guided by the central authority and local industry or of primary production by the relevant specialized Ministry. It also pertains, as it were, to decentralized production by other organizations for their own use and, on the other hand, to differing local conditions, relating specifically to the exploitation of raw material deposits. This includes, for example, the pronounced price differences for other building materials. Jasny says of these: "The costs of building materials produced by the building organizations themselves are normally higher, even much higher, than the prices to be paid to the State industry. During the early postwar years, this cost was up to threefold the prices charged by the state industry." He cites as reason for this the subsidies that are paid to the main producers subordinated to the relevant Union ministry. In addition there are the natural cost disadvantages of decentralized auxiliary output. "Being continually urged to fulfill their plans for construction in spite of the unavailability of building materials produced by the state industry, the construction organizations had, and have, no choice but to produce their own, without adequate equipment and on too small a scale —in effect, at any cost. . . ." [96, 97]

Out of the mixing of material and financial guidance methods, especially the material setting of production goals combined with financial regulation of the allocation of expense items, as shown in the preceding chapter, a strained condition develops among enterprisers that forces them to obtain by recourse to illegal ways the necessary input items for plan fulfillment, including labor supply, not obtainable through normal channels. Consequently, in State "markets" for producers' goods conditions analogous to black markets develop. This naturally affects costs and ultimately prices, as is shown in the following section. This strained condition is on the one hand an inducement to apply the scarcity principle in price formation, even against the will of the central planning authorities. On the other, it contributes to further confusion of relationships and hence to irrationalize the price system.

Because of the failure to think through the measures employed, only partial carrying out of these measures, and the application of contradictory principles, price-setting in the Soviet Union as a whole necessarily becomes unsystematic and fragmentary. In addition, a simple confusion and irrationality prevails in wide areas that are unexplainable on the basis of contradictory principles, but either on administrative awkwardness of price-setting agencies or on defects in their organization. Thus Baykov observes: "In 1939 it was emphasized that there existed different prices for similar products, not only in different regions but in one and the same region. There was no apparent cause for this, except the confusion that existed in the regulation of prices. Very often prices hampered rather than stimulated the production and improvement of range of goods." [98]

The irrationality and confusion are expressed primarily in the arbitrary, unexplainable deviations of prices from prime costs which, at times, move in opposite directions for closely related products and frequently assume bizarre proportions. Schwartz states: "Rates of profit on individual commodities also vary widely. Thus, in early 1938, spare parts for autos were bringing the automobile industry about 39 per cent profit, while spare parts for tractors were bringing the tractor industry a profit in excess of 150 per cent. Rubber shoes were bringing in an average profit of about 200 per cent, but auto tires were being sold at an average loss of 30 per cent. Some farm machines were sold for 25 per cent over cost; others were sold at a loss. In the cotton textile industry, some products were sold for profits of 20 to 30 per cent, while others were sold at losses ranging up to 10 to 15 per cent." [99, 100]

Here and there some special reasons for certain irrationalities in price setting may be observed. One of these, referred to in the preceding chapter, is the occasional delegation of authority to lower agencies to set prices. This pertains particularly to setting prices of new products for short periods following their initial production, and of products and productive services for which no wholesale prices have been authorized by the government, including price-setting by so-called interfirm cooperatives, i.e., contractual production or processing of parts of products by another enterprise. In all such cases, the right to set prices rests with the ministries, who, however, handle it "irresponsibly." For example, they do not approach the interested top buyer of products and productive services in advance, leave price-setting to chief administrations and even to separate enterprises, and do not examine these price-settings or the bases of their computation, nor control the maintenance of these prices. The lower agencies abuse the freedom thus available to improve their financial operating results. This occurs, in the first place, by simply setting excessively large profit mark-ups. Majzenberg gives illustrations of intrafirm cooperatives with profit rates of from 53 to 66 per cent.[101] In addition, there is the indirect way of inflating costs, especially of shifting costs. Enterprises in general are inclined to add as many expenditures as possible to noncomparable products, i.e., to new products and individually processed items, instead of to prices and costs of controlled, comparable products. Since as a rule the temporary price of a newly introduced product also appears to become the final price that is set, it is possible to cause considerable distortion in the price system in certain branches. This observation appears to attain considerable importance in the machine-building industries where newly introduced products always had decided significance, and for which Jasny designates as characteristic the disproportionate price spurts from time to time, with the appearance of new products.[102]

The Significance of Inflation for the Formation of the Soviet Price System

A further factor now to be discussed has considerable significance for the occasional formation of the price system. We shall first return to the question: What principles determine the height of the turnover tax and of planned profit, and particularly, are they instrumentalities with whose aid prices are regulated?

Detailed discussion has centered especially around the question of whether the turnover tax is such an instrument. Baykov, Dobb, Bettelheim, Sučkov, and Gordin[103] assert such a function. Opposite views are expressed in the report of Cairncross and by Joan Robinson.[104] The deliberation (by Cairncross) states unequivocally that, for consumers' goods and other products burdened with the turnover tax, both turnover tax and planned profit must be regarded as regulating instruments, aside from occasional cost manipulations; but for the mass of producers' goods (paying no turnover tax), only planned profit or loss is introduced and then only insofar as price regulation is intended to serve a definite setting of goal. Since no such regulation is carried out in principle, but only sporadically, a corresponding sporadic employment of the indicated instruments results, which helps to explain the contradictory assertions. Accordingly, support for both points of view can be found.[105] Nor should we expect too much systematic procedure in the choice of the regulating instrument, when both are concerned.

However, something further may be said about this problem. The key is given in the question of the elasticity of the separate price elements, in relation to each other and to the prices themselves. One might assume that these elasticities are the same, since regulation instrument and regulated object must undergo a parallel change. But such is not the case. The reason lies in a phenomenon that has been of fundamental significance for the development of the Soviet financial system thus far and has been worked out especially by Jasny; namely, the concurrence of rigid prices and fluctuating costs. Thus far we had not allowed for the fact that financially the Soviet economy has been in a stormy developmental period. The system is dynamic from three views. First, there is the dynamics of the cost structure, of productivity relationships, as a result of the rapid technological development, and the perfecting of the productive apparatus. Secondly, as a result of this industrialization, stimulation of the demand structure develops, permitting imposing on the economy—enormously strengthened in its productive power—entirely new tasks stemming from either the side of private consumption or the sphere of State purposes. Finally, there is an independent dynamic financial system. Since the beginning of the thirties, the country has been in an almost constant condition of inflation, and this last point, together with the first, is of particular significance in this connection.

This inflation appears unambiguously in the constant parallel upward movement of the mass of prices and average nominal wages.[106] The accompanying table indicates the development of the average annual nominal wage.[107]

AVERAGE ANNUAL NOMINAL WAGE

Year	Rubles	Index
1928	703	100
1932	1427	203
1935	2269	322.7
1938	3467	483.2
1940	4054	576.6
1946 (beginning of)	5250 or less	746.8
1946 (end of)	6500	924.6
1948	7056	1003.7
1950 (planned goal)	6000	853.5

An index of cost-of-living prices in Moscow State stores may serve to illustrate the simultaneous advance of prices.

Schwartz has computed this by combining two series of indexes prepared by different authors.[108]

COST-OF-LIVING PRICE INDEX

Year	Index
1928	100
1932	201
October 1935	806
1938	858
January 1941	1180
January 1948	2954
March 1950	2068

In general, it can be established that from about 1930 until 1948, with some reservation as to the years 1935 to 1938, continuous inflation prevailed. Apparently it has been possible to stop inflation since 1949-50, and even to permit a policy of lowering prices to take its place.[109]

The cause of inflation was the great need of the State for investment purposes and subsequently also for armament and defense, and later for war purposes. It is questionable how far this was planned, i.e., consciously taken into consideration from the beginning, and how far it came about unwanted because of nonfulfillment of plans. Jasny is of the opinion that the latter was the case. "Everyone was urged not only to fulfill but to overfulfill his goal. With State enterprises competing for goods and especially for labor, the goals for raising nominal wages were usually fulfilled, while the goals for increasing labor productivity—tied in with the wage goals by the plans (whose fulfillment, as a whole, depended on attainment of labor-productivity goals) —were reached only partially or failed altogether. The outcome was rising nominal outlays for labor per given product rather than the planned declines. The rising wages in the face of shortfalls of goals for labor productivity made inflation inevitable.[110] Complaints still continue as to the nonadherence to the planned relationship of wage outlays and quantity of output. Thus Finance Minister Zverev said in this 1954 budget message: "In connection with defects in labor organization and in the utilization of technique, building organizations permitted excess expenditures out of the labor wage fund, in comparison with the amount of work performed, by infringing on labor norms and prices." [111, 112]

This agrees with what was said above about the status of labor forces in the planning system, concerning the futile attempts to realize the requisite performance with the aid of legal compulsion alone. For this independent attitude of labor forces was a basic reason for the inability to compel adherence to the planned relationship between input and output. For example, Maljugin and Pisarevskij report: "Under present conditions, . . . fluctuation in the labor forces is simply unbearable. In January, workers, who had acquired expert building knowledge in the past months, wander away from building projects; with the beginning of the second quarter attempts are made to replace them, usually with people who first have to be trained. That must naturally affect the progress of plan fulfillment and the economic labor indexes of the building organizations. The number of workers who do not fulfill their labor norms increases, the wage fund is exceeded, expenses rise, and building schedules are not adhered to." [113]

It should be added that this situation not only made it impossible to enforce adherence to labor norms in the labor market, but also resulted directly in a continued unplanned increase in effective wage rates.[114] For example, enterprises bracketed workers in higher wage schedules and raised wages, or gave them more favorable norms in the piece-rate system.[115] The absurd consequence, which is now being criticized, was that workers in the highest wage bracket, particularly foremen, were hit hardest by the official upper wage limit, and now their compensation no longer stands in the proper relationship to that of the other workers.[116]

Even as wages, so also other expenditure items were increased, contrary to plan; for example, self-production of building materials not obtainable otherwise by building organizations regardless of costs, and the transporting of many goods by horse and wagon, for want of regular means of transportation.[117] Some idea can be gotten of the manner in which such increased costs are possibly passed on from enterprise to enterprise when one hears of the illegal addenda in contracts between State enterprises. These extend from buyers assuming expenditures that should be borne by the supplier to granting uncalculated counterservices (delivery of coal, wood, fuel), paying for services not rendered yet added to the labor bill, all the way to direct payment of overcharges (*Überpreisen*).[118]

After costs and prices had been set in motion in this manner, it became unavoidable for official wage rates to follow with further legalized wage increases, again with repercussions on costs and prices.[119] For the war period we may assume inflationary financing of public expenditure for Russia as well as for other countries engaged in war (by abandoning coverage of public outlays out of ordinary revenues, in the broader sense).

The fact that the items in the Soviet financial planning system displayed an over-all rather rapid upward movement during the observed period instead of oscillating around certain average values, which would be considered the normal case, explains to a large extent the indicated absurdities in the development of the price system. A price system moving in such a manner makes impossible maintaining the internal coordination, according to stated principles. Such coordination is conceivable only as a gradual process of mutual adjustment and balancing, and if the items to be coordinated in the meantime are moved by other forces, its basis is removed.

The manner in which this absurdity becomes apparent follows from the adjustment laws relating to individual price elements, partly because of inflation and partly for other reasons. From what has been said, inflation as such spontaneously affects prime costs, in that first wages per unit of product and then other cost items not controllable by the central authority are constantly pushed upward. This continuous upward movement of *costs** contrasts with relatively rigid *prices.** As has been shown, technical planning reasons necessitate holding reasonably stable numerical and particularly price data serving the economic planning and developmental process. This is because such data are so extensive and because the managerial apparatus using them is so complex that every larger change in their performance requires considerable time, and impairs the smooth functioning of the process during the interval. Frequent changes (of prices) could cause considerable confusion in such a situation. For adjustment (of prices to costs) these infrequent price changes must have a wide range; they must cover the distance covered by costs in many small steps with a few large leaps.

Since costs and prices are obviously related to each other, their different rhythm of movement must be removed by corrective changes in the latter (prices), by adjusting the tax factor as a fractional part of price. Of the two com-

* Italics supplied by editor of translation.

ponents of the tax factor (turnover tax and planned profits), only the turnover tax has a certain legal status of its own as to its change. Turnover tax rates are set, in essence, by central authorities. The same basic problem with which we become familiar in connection with pricing pertains to changes in them. Actually they appear to be somewhat more elastic than do prices. Jasny states: "Still, turnover taxes were changed more frequently than prices. They were a more elastic implement for adjustments than the latter." [120] But that is only a difference in degree. Such rates, established in advance, cannot achieve running correlation (of costs and prices). Only individual adjustment may be undertaken with their aid. The actual equilibrating medium must be the other part of the tax factor, planned profit. The function of planned profit corresponds with that of unplanned profit, insofar as the extent of planned profit (or possibly planned loss), not compensated for in specific cases by possible changes of prices or turnover tax, indicates changes in annual established new planned costs, while owing to cost changes the extent of unplanned profit or loss appears in the course of the year.

If this line of reasoning is correct, the characteristic of planned profit is not that of a positive component of price but a residual amount which, in its development, is determined by the internal legality governing the formation of the cost magnitudes. This makes its separation from the turnover tax intelligible. The turnover tax is the unconditionally planned medium for estimating and collecting the tax share of price, while planned profit, although fixed from year to year according to plan, is nevertheless exposed far more to action of arbitrary spontaneous developments within the price and finance system. The reasons given previously for separating them are not so much psychological and financial—technical, as they sound—but they also have a meaningful economic background. At the same time, the previously cited irrationalities in measuring planned profit are explained, for it is in the size of the residual that the consequences of rapid changes of all financial magnitudes and the resultant unavoidable irrationalities preventing coordination must become apparent.

Likewise the distribution of planned profits is explained, contrary to the intentions of the central authority. Increases in wage payments that represent the chief factor in inflation affect prices on the side of supply as a cost factor and, on the other hand, on the side of demand. On the supply side, where in principle this effect is distributed uniformly over all economic areas, it was easier to yield to this pressure in setting prices of consumers' goods than of means of production, on which the attention of planners was primarily focused, and to which all that was previously said as to the interest in maintaining price stability for technical planning reasons pertains. But the pressure on the side of demand affected price formation of consumers' goods almost exclusively, whereas, on the contrary, lower prices were sought in the case of producers' goods because of vague conceptions of the possible support here. All this led to the readiness to make liberal price adjustments of consumers' goods oftener and quicker. Hence, planned profits, in general, had to be larger here. Indeed, a contradictory developmental tendency became apparent in that the dynamics of costs, operating toward creating losses in producers' goods production, rather created the presumption of increasing profit. To be sure, their realization in specific instances depended on the prevailing very inelastic price policy of the central agency. But, in general, the division of the economy into an excessively profitable consumer goods sector and a strongly subsidized producer goods sector plagued with losses has become reality, as was to be expected.

The picture that Jasny presents of the development of the Soviet price system, especially of prices of producers' goods, during the past 25 years fully agrees with these observations.[121]

Final Evaluation of the Price System

In conclusion, an attempt must now be made to evaluate the Soviet price system comprehensively. Such an evaluation is a difficult undertaking in many respects, hence it must be made with certain reservations.

The point of view from which it will be judged centers in the question: How far has it succeeded in establishing the internal consistency of the valuation system, so that the money units assigned to goods express their actual significance in the sense of desired economic goals? Thus an absolute measure of value is applied to the price system. But judgment so expressed says nothing as to the quality and suitability of this price system as compared with another empirically given system, such as that commonly called the market economy in Western countries, very much simplified. Such a comparison of empirically given price systems, which actually aims at comparing guidance systems, cannot be made with the materials here presented. In particular, an examination into the degree of rationality of the actual Western price system is lacking; it is usually assumed hastily that all is well if "competition" prevails. Moreover, the price system is but one of the indicators with the aid of which the performance potential of a guidance system can be judged. In general, every guidance system must be judged in relation to the historical background of a country, its mental attitudes, its educational status, the trend in the education of the people and particularly of the ruling class, together with the condition under which the system was developed and the purposes it is to serve. In this connection, it must be reiterated, the purposes served by any guidance system have no other meaning for judging it than its suitability to test the realization of indicated objectives that have been adopted. Evaluation of goals has nothing to do with evaluation of the guidance system.

A further reservation results from the kind of materials used. The starting point of the presentation shows an internal break in the consistency of the guidance system developed as officially valid. The practical consequences of this break, the resultant limits of validity of the system, must be inferred from an abundance of individual statements and references and especially from criticisms directed against "mistakes" in practice. That practical significance is attached to these deviations from the system can be seen in the consideration given them by developing legal regulations, not only negative as prohibitions but also positive, by seeking to use the innate effectiveness of forces and movements to attain the guidance objectives. Naturally, it is impossible on the basis of available material to comprehend the quantitative significance of the deviations in economic practice, its actual importance relative to its importance in the initial system and in comparison with current economic processes, nor in how far forces adverse to the system are integrated by alterations to make it serve goals set by the central authority and in how far they remain disturbing elements. We may recognize effective formative tendencies, but can scarcely evaluate them in their relative significance to each other.

We can thus establish the fact that because of its economic peculiarities and significance the Soviet price system cannot be labeled unequivocally with a short caption such as "irrationality," "political profitability," "functional use of the price mechanism." Abolition of subsidies, emphatically proclaimed twice, cannot be taken as a turning point in the development of the Soviet planning system, much as one should like to do so. Jasny comments on the transition to the "functional use of the price mechanism" that Kaser thought he detected in 1949: "However, there has been much talk of this for a long time, but thus far the good intentions could not be realized. The measures taken in 1948-49 represent neither something new nor a definite turn." [122] Furthermore, we can establish the fact that the basic decision in favor of functional use of the price mechanism to construct a thoroughly coordinated price system based on the evidence function of money (see Chapter 2, p. 46), has by no means been made. Rather the negative attitude toward the thought of financial economic guidance prevails theoretically, and the transition to financial guidance takes place without discussion of principle, but solely out of the requirements of planning practice. Obviously, such a change, growing out of the requirements and stimuli of practice, progresses but slowly and cannot develop into a completely equitable system as long as hostility to it maintains theoretical supremacy.

If now we evaluate in detail the results attained thus far, we must conclude, first, that the chief disturbing factor in the Soviet price system has been inflation. It was recognized as such, and effort was made to get rid of it shortly after the first years of large-scale construction, in 1936. This attempt has been repeated with even greater clarity of objective, as soon as time could be found for a calm, progressive development of the planning system after the confusion of the war years and the urgent problems of the first postwar period. In case these efforts have been successful, they have provided a first prerequisite for rationalizing the price system. As indicated, not sufficient corroborative material is available to me to determine their success.

Furthermore, we say that while only direct and indirect payment for labor is considered in costs, and not payments for other primary factors of production, nevertheless the tendency exists throughout to develop the relative costs (the wage relationships) according to the scarcity conditions of this factor. A distortion of these cost relationships by taxes occurs, to a significant extent, only in case of consumers' goods. Here, in spite of individual attempts to consider consumer preference in production and distribution, the shaping of the price system in accordance with the preferences of consumers is not spoken of favorably.[123] However, as shown in the first chapter, the actually significant goals of Soviet economic planning do not lie in the field of consumer wants, but in the area of State objectives; its primary concern relates to price formation of producers' goods. These, as we have seen, are almost entirely free from turnover tax; where a turnover tax is here collected, it is apparently either a case of considering conditions of particular scarcity not finding expression in labor costs or indirectly to influence distribution,[124] whose financial significance is presumably greater than the losses arising out of price distortion. As far as the relation of costs to prices is concerned (including amounts of turnover tax, determined according to particular planning objectives), removal of inflation was combined every time with the effort to establish their normal relationship by removing the irrational profit margins and subsidies.[125] This view also makes the recently recommended normal profit margin significant.

Finally, we also saw that direct regulation of prices based on conditions of scarcity by raising them to encourage production and restrict consumption, and conversely by lowering them to encourage consumption, does occur extensively. A combination of these two tendencies would be possible only if, in regulating the quantity of output, financial criteria were considered, and thus lead to very close approach to the optimal price system. In general, it can be said that at least in as far as price formation of producers' goods is concerned, there are pronounced tendencies toward rational formation of the price system in the Soviet Union.

On the other hand, these are merely *tendencies** and not a basically developed, preponderatingly effective principle of price formation. These tendencies still conflict everywhere with other pricing principles or simply with lack of insight. Nor is it at all certain that abolition of subsidies has actually been carried out, and that the principle of irrational preferential treatment in price formation has finally been abolished. Conversely, we may assume that consideration of scarcity conditions in price regulation occurs only when they have actually led to maladjustments that cannot be overlooked, and there also other steps for making corrections are taken.

Furthermore, even where the problem is attacked correctly, as we saw, a certain lack of coordination as well as an incorrect and excessive use of particularized measures is due to the absence of theoretical insight into the nature and consequences of what is desired. Above all, the measures taken cannot be systematically coordinated because of lack of insight into the problem they actually pose, relative to two points. First, there is the absence or rejection of the marginal cost concept—prices that are based on average

* Italics supplied by editor of translation.

costs and in addition neglect certain cost factors entirely cannot correctly indicate over-all economic scarcities, and every consideration of such scarcity relationships in price must again open up gaps between costs and prices (if based on average costs). The previously cited illustrations in which inequalities in cost levels for the same or related goods, indicated in prices, produce distortions in the entire financial coordination system, indicate that this point is not merely of academic significance. Secondly, even more important is the wrong starting point, where the financial guidance criteria become effective. These should actually influence drawing up of the plan, and hence be considered by all agencies of the guidance system, primarily by the higher agencies, which make the more fundamental decisions. Instead they influence chiefly the lowest agencies, the enterprises, and especially in addition to or contrary to the plan. Thus is brought about that internal strained relationship between the material and the financial planning system that we observed previously. This is especially damaging to the internal consistency of the guidance system.

In evaluating all these conditions—assuming that inflation will finally be checked, and furthermore, the road taken thus far will be pursued further—the over-all Soviet price system gives evidence of the relative significance of the appraised items in terms of the evidence function (of money) even though it is impossible to consider it a closely coordinated value system.

Footnotes and References

Chapter 1

1. According to L. Wolodarski, "Planning in the Economic and Cultural Reconstruction in the Soviet Union" (G tr. from R), Berlin, 1947, pp. 17 f., 20 f.
2. Charles Bettelheim, *The Soviet Economy* (F), Paris, 1950, pp. 436-441.
3. According to Harry Schwartz, *Russia's Soviet Economy*, New York, 1950, p. 157.
4. J. Joffe, "Planning Industrial Production" (G tr. from R). Supplement to *Soviet Economy* (G), Berlin, 1949, p. 103.
5. Schwartz, *op. cit.*, p. 168.
6. Compare, for example, the formulation of guiding objectives and limits for the second Five-Year Plan, in V. V. Obolensky-Ossinsky, "Planning in the Soviet Union," in *Foreign Affairs*, 1934/35, Vol. 13, pp. 456 f., or statements as to production goals, in particular the planned growth coefficients in the second, third, and fourth Five-Year Plans by Maurice Dobb, *Soviet Economic Development since 1917*, 2d ed. London, 1951, pp. 268 ff., 292 f., 306 ff., et al.
7. An illustration of such a balance is given by N. S. Margolin, *Balance of Monetary Income and Expenditures of the Population* (R), Moscow, 1951, pp. 61 ff., and by Alexander Baykov, *The Development of the Soviet Economic System*, Cambridge, 1946; New York, 1947, pp. 476-479.
8. Margolin, *op. cit.*, pp. 43 f.
9. *Ibid.*, pp. 41 f., 62 ff.
10. *Ibid.*, pp. 130-135.
11. Baykov, *op. cit.*, pp. 256, 457.
12. This observation is significant for the subsequent investigation, particularly as to the applicability of our rationality criterion to Russian economic planning.
13. To confirm this opinion, compare particularly the list of ministries, given for example by Schwartz, *op. cit.*, pp. 174 f. (as of June, 1950) and observe that hitherto industrial branches in which primarily new construction is taking place have been managed solely by all-Union ministries.

14. See below, "Norms as Routine Stimulation of the Economy."
15. Illustrations of such balances are reproduced in many places, such as the cited works by Schwartz, Bettelheim, and Joffe.
16. According to Baykov, *op. cit.,* pp. 431, 443 f., 440 f., 444 ff.; et al.
17. According to E. Lokšin, "Questions as to Planning Technical Raw Material Requirements of the Economy of the U.S.S.R." (R), *Planned Economy,* No. 2, p. 46, reproduced by Schwartz, *op. cit.,* pp. 161 f.
18. David Granick, *Management of the Industrial Firm in the U.S.S.R.,* New York, 1954, pp. 135 ff.
19. B. Glusker, P. Krylov, "As to the Index Numbers System of Economic Planning" (R), in *Planned Economy,* 1954, No. 5, pp. 80-86; et al.
20. A. Kurski, "Planning of the Economy in the USSR" (G tr. of R), Moscow, 1949, pp. 99 f., 105 f.; et al.
21. *Ibid.,* p. 117. E. Lokšin, "Norming of Material Input in Production" (R), in *Planned Economy,* 1950, No. 6, p. 87.
22. Illustrations in Joffe, *op. cit.,* pp. 88 f.; et al.
23. *Ibid.,* pp. 92 f., 64 f., 67f.
24. Number of workers required for a given production program is computed as follows: Norm time per unit of product, times annual output task divided by annual labor time per worker. Cf. M. Jampol'skij, "Labor Planning" (R), in *Planned Economy,* No. 5 (1951), pp. 87 f.; et al.
25. The campaign was opened with Stalin's address at the first all-Union Congress of Stakhanov Workers in 1935. The manner of computation is arranged so that the arithmetical average norms of achievements of Stakhanovites are not permitted to become effective as incentive to all workers, while norms based on highest attained values are not adapted to the general level of achievement, and hence are unrealistic. Cf. N. Fedotov, "Progressive Average Norms," "Principles of Planning Production" (R), in *Planned Economy,* 1949, No. 3, p. 37.
26. The literature pertaining to the question of progressive

norms is very extensive. Cf. for example M. N. Grunkin, *Intra-Concern Chozrasčet and the Introduction of Progressive Norms* (R). Moscow, 1950 (best source!), et al.

27. M. Michajlov, "As to Reserves of Prime Cost Reduction in Industrial Production" (R), in *Planned Economy,* 1953, No. 2, p. 53.

28. A well-balanced presentation of the Stakhanovite problem is given by Granick, *op. cit.,* pp. 243-252; cf. also Baykov, *op. cit.,* pp. 337 ff.

29. The plans contain aggregative norms for projected increased productivity and lower costs. Cf. for example G. Bienstock, S. M. Schwarz, A. Yugow, *Management in Russian Industry and Agriculture,* London, New York, Toronto, 1944, pp. 72 ff.; et al.

30. It should be added that such an aimless pressure to lower costs is more meaningful in Russia than elsewhere, since opportunities for savings in costs by means of improved organizational details are still very considerable there. Cf. Dobb, *op. cit.,* pp. 429-432; et al.

31. Joffe, *op. cit.,* pp. 92 ff.

32. Conversely, investment planning in practice in our Western "capitalistic" economy does not follow exclusively the "commercial speculative" principle here indicated. The comparison of these two methods is therefore not to serve the purpose of an over-all characterization of a market and a planned economic system.

33. L. Berri, K. Klimenko, "The Mechanization of Labor Intensive Processes in the Industry of the Soviet Union" (R), in *Problems of Economics,* No. 3, 1949, pp. 17-32; et al.

34. A. Zacharov, V. Oligin, "Progressive Norms and Mobilization of Internal Reserves of Production" (R) in *Planned Economy,* 1953, No. 2, p. 67.

35. V. D'jačenko, "Khozraschet as Socialist Economic Method" (R), in *Problems of Economics,* 1951, No. 2, p. 10.

36. E. Lokšin, "Norming of Material Input in Production" (R), in *Planned Economy,* No. 6 (1950), pp. 88 ff.

37. In May 1955 the previous "State Planning Committee" (*Gosplan,* until 1948 State Planning Commission) was divided into a commission for current planning and a commission for long-term planning ("Perspective Planning") of the economy, which now alone is called *Gosplan.* The new *Gosplan* now merely draws up five-year plans and long-term perspective plans. Coordinating and balancing in drawing up annual plans as well as their breakdown into quarterly plans is now the problem of the commission for current planning. (Cf. R. W. Davies, *The Reappraisal of Industry, op. cit.,* pp. 310 ff., 313 f.). In the text the designation *Gosplan* has been retained, since the presentation pertains primarily to the period prior to 1955. Actually, the two new planning commissions must remain closely related in their work, since long-term plans can be worked out only on the bases derived from current plans, but again form the connecting basis for drawing up annual plans.

38. Thus far, according to Bettelheim, *op. cit.,* pp. 425 f., et al. Somewhat different is the picture drawn by Joffe (*op. cit.,* pp. 31-36, 61). However, his statements are too indefinite to permit a correction of the other authors. The concept "directives" is ambiguous, since partly it indicates only the instructions given to *Gosplan* by the Party and the government, and partly also the draft of the plan, which begins its journey downward from *Gosplan.* This difference is presumably explained by the development of the participation in planning by *Gosplan,* indicated subsequently, and hence by the nature of its "directives" transmitted further.

39. According to the somewhat limited reference in Baykov, *op. cit.,* p. 457.

40. *Ibid.,* p. 457.

41. The Peoples' Council of Commissaries.

42. "Norming," *op. cit.,* pp. 87 f.

Chapter 2

1. Instead of many references, cf. G. Kozlov, J. V. Stalin as to Commodity Production and the Law of Value under Socialism (R), *Communist*, Moscow, 1952, No. 31. (G) in *Soviet Science*, Social Section, 1953, pp. 3, 11, 20 f.; et al.

2. The expressions "financial," "financial planning," etc. are not used here in the special sense, "relating to the State budget," "State budget planning," etc., but generally in the sense of "pecuniary economic planning," "planning in monetary terms," in contrast with "material economic planning," "planning in kind."

3. The way in which this is possible and within what limitations will be examined more closely in the following chapter. "Relationship Between Determining Goal and Guiding Method."

4. The valuation of all purposes and means, the measurement of output quantities of every commodity and combination of input quantities of means of production needed for their output follows from the stated conditions, according to the known rules of marginal theory. The resultant value system corresponds with the description that Heinrich von Stackelberg has given of the competitive economic system in the last section of his *Principles* (*Principles of Theoretical Economic Doctrine*) (G), Bern, 1948, pp. 338-343, and also p. 346, if "fulfillment of purpose" is substituted for "utility," and "spending agency" for "budget," and the resultant necessary restatements are undertaken.

5. The purely instrumental interpretation of the price system has been developed primarily by socialists, who undertook a positive analysis of the problem of economic accounting and consequently were accused of inadmissible acceptance of liberal capitalistic concepts. I find this thought first expressed clearly by Lerner, who developed it in such an explanation with Maurice Dobb (cf. Maurice Dobb, "Economic Theory and the Problems of a Socialist Economy,"

in *Economic Journal,* Vol. 43, pp. 588-598; Abba P. Lerner and M. Dobb, "Economic Theory and Socialist Economy, with Reply and Rejoinder, in *Review of Economic Studies,* 1934-35, Vol. 11, pp. 51-61, 144-154); et al.

6. The general applicability of our price theory is also disputed from various angles and with diverse arguments. A discussion of the familiar argument of the Mises-Hayek-Eucken group that a purposive, coordinated price system can be created only by free exchange among independent market participants appears in the following chapter, "Compatibility of the Material and the Financial Guiding Method." The opposite or contrasting point of view is expressed by K. Paul Hensel in *Introduction to the Theory of the Centrally Administered Economy* (G), Stuttgart, 1954, which the author considers fundamentally fallacious.

7. The distinction here drawn between "evidence function" and "developmental and control function of money" does not coincide with the customary distinction made in monetary theory between measure of value (accounting unit) and medium of exchange.

8. For a planned economy with its economic entities directed toward common interests, enterprise *(Unternehmen)* is an unsuitable but unavoidable translation of *predprijatie;* some English authors translate the term "concern," "plants," "firm," or even "factory," but these appear too narrow in their connotation, hence the literal translation "enterprise" is used throughout the English rendition.

9. G. Bienstock, S. M. Schwarz, and A. Yugow, *Management in Russian Industry and Agriculture,* London, New York, Toronto, 1944, *op. cit.,* pp. 56 f.; Alexander Baykov, *The Development of the Soviet Economic System,* Cambridge, 1946, *op. cit.,* pp. 451-456; et al.

10. The threefold classification of goods in the system of distribution is described in the following chapter.

11. Thus far, according to R. O. Halfina, "Managerial Act and

Agreement" (R), exerpts in *Soviet Studies,* 1954-55, Vol. 5, especially pp. 93 ff.; et al.

12. Concerning this, see below, in this chapter, "Differing Attitude Toward Use of Financial Magnitudes as Lead Criteria."

13. Maurice Dobb, *Soviet Economic Development since 1917,* London, 1951, *op. cit.,* p. 382; R. W. Davies, "Short-term Credit in the U.S.S.R.; Some Post-War Problems," *Soviet Studies,* 1953-54, Vol. 5, p. 20, footnote 6.

14. Parenthetically, it should also be considered here that the material planning system is not fully worked out, but is gradually developed from rudimentary beginnings, simultaneously with the financial guidance system. See in this connection the references to the development of balances and norms in Chapter 1. However, this evolution of the material planning system does not take place at the expense of the financial planning system, but parallels it, and apparently is not intended to replace it.

15. Ostrovitjanov, "Socialist Planning and the Law Value" (R) in *Problems of Economics,* 1948, No. 1 (G) tr. in *Soviet Science,* 1948, No. 2, p. 35.

16. Literally "economical accounting." The concept embraces the aggregate of pecuniary accounting and control processes, related to separate enterprises (as well as to "intraconcern *khozraschet*"), i.e., divisions, shops, and labor brigades. In the absence of a corresponding English concept, the Russian word *khozraschet* will be used throughout the translation.

17. M. M. Usoskin, *Organization and Planning Credit in the U.S.S.R.* (R), Moscow, 1951, p. 7.

18. A. Arakelian, *Industrial Management in the U.S.S.R.* (tr.) Washington, D.C., 1950, p. 92; et al.

19. See for example Baykov, *op. cit.,* pp. 220 ff., 348 ff.; et al.

20. Ostrovitjanov, *op. cit.,* pp. 29, 33 f.

21. *Ibid.,* p. 29.

22. Discussed below.

23. V. M. Batyrev and V. K. Sitnin, *Organization and Planning of the Finances of Socialist Industry* (R), Gosplan Publishing House, 1940, p. 43; et al.

24. Development of their own fund is well presented by Poom, "Economy, Effectiveness and Profitability in Soviet Industry" (G), in *Journal for Commercial Science Research*, 1952, New Series, Vol. 4, pp. 198-222. According to V. D'jačenko, "The Objective Bases of Khozraschet" (R), in *Problems of Economics*, 1956, Vol. 1, p. 7, the Director's Fund has been renamed "Fund of the enterprise to improve the living conditions of the workers, and to perfect production." For sake of brevity, "Director's Fund" is used throughout the translation.

25. Harald Bräutigam, "Financial Planning, Authoritative Price Fixing and Capital Formation in the Soviet Union" (G), in *Yearbooks for National Economy and Statistics*, 1943, Vol. 158, p. 303.

26. V. Lipsic, "Ways to Improve Planning of Prime Costs of Industrial Production" (R), *Planned Economy*, 1952, No. 3, pp. 31 f.: et al.

27. L. M. Kantor, S. D. Ratner, I. S. Suderevskij in "Organization of Intra-Firm Khozraschet" (R), (G) *op. cit.*, pp. 67-72, 77 ff.

28. Usoskin, *op. cit.*, p. 10.

29. The presentation is very much simplified, and is not a picture of reality but of the principles pertaining to a system, still in the developmental stage, according to Usoskin, *op. cit.*, pp. 10, 52, 55 (particularly pp. 57 ff.) etc.

    Moreover, there are complaints that banks do not exercise control according to instructions; thus Lavrov complains "that in extending credit, the necessary distinction is not drawn between enterprises, which fulfill the drawn-up plans, and those which do not fulfill the plans, which incur losses, and have larger supplies of material values, than correspond with set norms." (V. Lavrov, "Ruble Control in the National

Economy" (R), in *Planned Economy,* 1953, No. 5, pp. 63 f., 67 f.)

30. *Ibid.,* pp. 60 f.
31. Baykov, *op. cit.,* pp. 373 ff; Naum Jasny, *The Soviet Price System,* Stanford, 1951, p. 77 as well as Appendix, Table 1, pp. 166 f.
32. Minimum turnover tax rates have been discontinued since 1949 (Jasny, *op. cit.,* p. 77). In general, profits tax rates have been raised, so that even the internally accumulated investment means of promoted industrial branches are now largely financed by the State budget.
33. V. D'jačenko, "Khozrashchet as Socialist Economic Method" (R), in *Problems of Economics,* 1951, No. 2, pp. 13, 17 f. (G in *Soviet Science,* 1951).
34. A. Bačurin, "Concerning Profitability in Socialist Industry" (R), in *Problems of Economics,* 1953, No. 4, p. 40.
35. A. Vorob'eva, according to *Soviet Studies,* Vol. 2, 1950, p. 97, et al.
36. A. Arakelian, *Industrial Management in the U.S.S.R., op. cit.,* p. 94.
37. Batyrev and Sitnin, *op. cit.,* p. 40.
38. This struggle is presented in detail by Dobb, *Soviet Economic Development Since 1917, op. cit.,* Ch. 8, pp. 177-207.
39. V. D'jačenko, "Stalin's New Work 'Economic Problems of Socialism in the U.S.S.R.' " (R), (G) in *Soviet Science,* 1952, p. 518, et al.

The simultaneously acknowledged "Influence of the Law of Value on Production" derives primarily from the necessity of money accounting instead of labor time accounting for control and stimulation in the usual sense. "The input of labor and measure of consumption are controlled under socialism in terms of value. This necessitates calculating expenditure of direct (*lebendiger*) and machine (*vergegenständlichter*) labor indirectly in terms of value. Stalin points out that consideration of the law of value by our managers has positive significance, since it trains them mentally to manage concerns rationally, to maintain discipline, and compels them to calculate volumes of production carefully. . . ." Kozlov, according to *Soviet Science, op. cit.,* pp. 13-14, et al.

40. Usoskin, *op. cit.,* p. 10.

41. Harry Schwartz, *Russia's Soviet Economy,* New York, 1950, *op. cit.,* p. 190.

42. J. Joffe, "Planning Industrial Production," *op. cit.,* p. 106.

43. S. Ja. Tureckij, *Prime Cost and Questions of Price Formation,* Gosplan Publishing House, 1940 (R), cited by Harold Bräutigam, "Financial Planning, Authoritarian Price Fixing and Capital Formation in the Soviet Union" (G), in *Yearbook for National Economy and Statistics,* 1943, Vol. 158, pp. 283 f.

44. According to B. Mirošničenko, "Planning Industrial Production" (R), in *Planned Economy,* 1951, No. 3; excerpts in *Soviet Studies,* 1951-52, Vol. 3, p. 440.

45. *Ibid.* p. 440.

46. I.e., purchasing divisions.

47. A. Vorob'eva, according to *Soviet Studies,* Vol. 2, 1950/51, *op. cit.,* pp. 102, 106.

48. Batyrev and Sitnin, *op. cit.,* p. 41.

49. *Ibid.,* p. 42; cf. also A. Vorob'eva (*Soviet Studies,* Vol. 2, 1950/51 *op. cit.,* p. 102). "Prices of waste and by-products should be much lower than those of basic materials, and should stimulate their maximum utilization in the enterprise or for sale." More specific quotations and further material relating to all this are given in "Viewpoints of Price Regulation," Chapter 4.

50. J. V. Stalin, "New Relationships—New Problems of Economic Construction" (R), 1931 address, reprinted in *Problems of Leninism,* 11th ed. Moscow, 1939. German translation, 1946 (pp. 402 ff. Section VI, as to the profitability principle, pp. 418 ff., especially 420 ff.

51. J. V. Stalin, 1933, Report to the plenary session of the

Central Committee as to the first Five Year Plan, reprinted in *Problems of Leninism;* (G tr.), *op. cit.,* pp. 462 f. The closing statement is often quoted.

52. A. Arakelian, *op. cit.,* p. 84.
53. Ostrovitjanov, "Socialist Planning and the Law of Value" (R), in *Problems of Economics,* No. 1, 1948; (G), *Soviet Science* 1948, No. 2, p. 51.
54. P. Orlov and J. Romanov, "The Question of Methodology of Comparing Variations in Projected Structures" (R), *Problems of Economics,* 1951, No. 1, p. 108.
55. G. Levin, "Questions of Determining Economic Suitability of Planning Decisions" (R), *Problems of Economics,* 1950, No. 4, pp. 76, 77 f.; cf. also p. 81 as well as the reservation on p. 72, etc.
56. V. D'jačenko, "Stalin's New Work," (R), *op. cit.,* p. 314.
57. D. Černomordik, "The Utility Effect of Capital Investments and the Theory of Reproduction" (R), *Problems of Economics,* 1949, No. 6; (G), *Soviet Science,* 1949, No. 3, p. 20.
58. As to the excessive favoring of consumer's goods industries relative to the attack on profits see Batyrev and Sitnin, *op. cit.,* pp. 37, 43 f.
59. This system and reasons for it are dealt with in detail subsequently.

Chapter 3

1. The decentralized, financially guided economy may thus be an exchange economy, a free enterprise economy, as well as a socialist economy, in which power to make decisions by management does not depend on property and contract but on instituting it by political authority. Such a "competitive socialist system" has now been developed by several authors, most consistently by Oscar Lange ("On the Economic Theory of Socialism," in *Review of Economic Studies,* Vol. IV, 1936/37). As to the history of the dogma, compare Edward Herman, "Concerning the History of the Theory

of Socialist Economy" (G), in Herman, *Socialist Economic and Social Order,* new ed. 1948, pp. 62-86 (first appeared in *Social Research,* 1939); et al.

2. Walter Eucken, *Principles of Political Economy* (G), 5th ed. Godesberg, 1947, pp. 127, 131, 138 ff., 199 f.; et al.

3. Ostrovitjanov "Socialist Planning and the Law of Value," *op. cit.,* p. 24.

4. Cf. the types of centrally managed economies in Euken, *Principles, op. cit.,* pp. 130-137; et al.

5. *Ibid.,* p. 139; cf. also footnote 32, p. 399.

6. K. Paul Hensel, *Introduction to the Theory of the Centrally Managed Economy* (G), Stuttgard, 1954, pp. 113 ff.

7. *Ibid.,* pp. 146 f., et al.

8. Walter Eucken, "Temporal Guidance of the Economic Process and Construction of Economic Orders" (G), in *Yearbooks for Political Economy and Statistics,* Vol. 159, 1944 pp. 182 ff.; et al.

9. See above, Chapter 2, Economic Sense of Money Calculation."

10. Eucken, "Temporal Guidance," *op. cit.,* pp. 188-193; et al.

11. With subsequently presented reservation.

12. Cf. Chap. 1, "Participation of Central and Lower Agencies in Drawing up the Plan."

13. With him it is essentially both a materially and financially guided economy; cf. *Principles, op. cit.,* pp. 128-30, 143 f.

14. *Ibid.,* p. 137.

15. In this connection central guidance is understood to mean material (guidance) and "decentralized" guidance, financial.

16. Hensel, *op. cit.,* pp. 71 ff., 112, 115-121, 210.

17. Community purposes may again be subdivided into those considered by the central political organization, the state, and those considered by separate local (*Teil*) governments (for example municipalities). What is said subsequently as to private demand may be applied by analogy to the latter; their fulfillment is ultimately the responsibility of the central political agency, it can either embody the individual

purposes directly in its purposive system or assign to the separate communities as lump-sum average quota ("income") to satisfy all demands, according to their roughly estimated relative importance.

18. Hans Ritschl in this connection, "The Theory of Political Science and Taxation" (G), (Bonn, *Pol. Sci. Investigations,* Vol. 11), Bonn and Leipzig, 1925, particularly pp. 150-157, 189-197, etc.

19. Cf. the cited work of Euken, *Principles;* et al.

20. In particular, separation of means for private consumption, in accordance with the judgment as to the importance of individually demanded items, such as separating means of serving collective purposes from those serving private use, is meaningless if the delimited means are then not used for the assumed purposes.

21. Cf. material distribution system with the aid of ration card coupons, as suggested by Ritschl (Hans Ritschl, "Principles of Collective Economy" (G), in *Research in Social Composition of the Economic Order,* Publication of the Society for Social Policy, Berlin, 1950, New Series, Vol. 2, pp. 26-28.

22. At the same time this helps to test summarily the demands of lower agencies as to suitability and realizability.

23. This includes a change of goals in the field of production of producers' goods: for example, decrease in the production of agricultural machinery with simultaneous increase in the production of fertilizers, always with the idea of substituting means if the interchanged means of production serve the same final purpose. Whether it is a case of substituting either means or ends can be decided only by an over-all survey of the economy, not from the standpoint of a single concern. Every substitution of means in one concern, not related to the "original factors of production," requires a "change of goal" for other producing concerns. The concepts "goals" and "substitution of means" appear frequently in Hensel, *op. cit.,* 18 ff.

24. Furthermore, substitution of material guidance has greater

significance for achieving balance than has financial guidance. That is because here the possibilities of substituting means is correspondingly less. For the possibilities of substituting means is correspondingly less. For the possibilities of substituting means, as such, are widely intertwined in a multiplicity of opportunities. Only a few are recognizable by the central agency. Since essential balancing measures in material guidance are taken only by the higher agencies, a large part of opportunities for substitution is here lost. To be sure, the area can be extended, by referring back to the lower agencies, with instructions, to seek possibilities of substitution in a certain direction. But this is no complete substitute for financial guidance, here afforded. Opportunities for indirect substitution are perhaps largely lost. It should be added, that introduction of financial valuation into the material guidance system, where possible, creates further potentialities. Cf. the following section.

25. For example, no one can say in advance that the first half pound of butter per week is worth 5 Mark to him, the second half-pound 3 Mark, and the third, 1 Mark; the first suit per year 300 Mark, the second, 125 Mark (with a given income and price level), and conclude that he wanted to buy a half pound of butter twice per week and one suit of clothes annually. But he will be able to establish, for example, that, with the prevailing condition of supply, a little more butter would be more important than sausage, or that the new suit of clothes is so important to him that he would rather cut down on food or smoking or somewhere else; or conversely, that in view of the high price of the suit such far-reaching retrenchments would be necessary that, in comparison with these, the suit would not be important enough, etc.

26. Joan Robinson, "Mr. Wiles' Rationality," a comment in *Soviet Studies*, 1955-56, Vol. 7, p. 273.

27. To be sure, aside from the market forms, since here we can limit ourselves to the rational guidance system.

28. Cf. the preceding chapter, "The Economic System of Money Calculation."

29. For all this, see Grunau "Rational Principle, Economic Accounting and Economic System" in *World Economic Archive*, Vol. 64, 1950, pp. 268-279.

30. It has been pointed out correctly that the publicly managed economy in a market-guided economic environment, which also illustrates public goal-setting represents a counterpart of the domestic economy of consumers, just examined, and not of the production economy, performing entirely with financial valuations. (Ritschl, *Principles of Collective Economy* (G), *op. cit.*, pp. 7 ff.).

31. To be sure, even this is questionable. Theory is working with a fiction, insofar as it assumes that individual acts of choice are necessarily compatible with each other, because they are consciously made.

32. It should be noted at once that this problem cannot be solved by decentralization of governmental functions, transferring them to a multiplicity of independent corporations with, so to say, their own income, analogous to the solution of the problem of freedom of choice of consumers. For the actual problem is an objective differentiation of demand, the over-all satisfaction of which is accomplished with the idea of general welfare in mind, no matter how interpreted, and hence must be coordinated from this point of view in all individual measures. Division of functions among independent agencies would actually negate this task; it would not even give an opportunity to consider all goals and to eliminate subterfuges. On the contrary, the problem of coordination also exists in like manner where public tasks are naturally performed by various public corporations. For the public corporations do not appear as individuals, entitled to income, but are common organizations for general welfare, where the fulfillment of all individual purposes must be carried out according to the coordinating central idea; an excess in fulfillment of purpose in the area of one

corporate body must therefore be balanced by a deficit in the area of another.

33. Which, in view of what has been cited above, must be material.

34. Or to every individual head in the executive body (*Gremium*) carrying out the coordination.

35. Should one want to insert financial magnitudes in the process of coordination of goals—which is conceivable only with centralized determination of goal—this would mean thus far abandoning the solution of the problem of coordination, and replacing it by a model. More about this below.

36. Naturally only if financial guidance methods are employed at all.

37. As already indicated, both tasks will obviously be fulfilled, in part, by the same apparatus. The two processes work together in the following manner: for every quantity decision reached, the relevant marginal costs are computed, and in case of deviations of exchange relationships from initially reached decisions as to choice, first determination of quantities and again the marginal costs are corrected alternately until they coincide. Because of the usual low price elasticity, particularly of public demand, the process should produce rapid convergence. To be sure, adjustments in the entire area of coordination are possible only in rare cases of particularly pronounced deviations, in view of the magnitude of the cumbersome apparatus.

38. In general, the central authority determines all or a very large part of the quantity of production, while the share of the individual consumer, as a rule, is insignificant in relation to the entire output.

39. For example, the consumer primarily wants 12 pounds of bread per week, which at prevailing prices cost about 5 Mark, not 5 Mark worth of bread, no matter how much that may be. Should the price change, the demanded quantity will eventually change, but the starting point of

the choices is not the household budgeted 5 Mark, but the planned quantity of consumption of 12 pounds.

40. In this case areas remain in which the State appears besides the private giver of orders, and (here) price retains its function as regulator of quantity, sometimes completely, sometimes at least at the outset.

41. This also holds true where the orders of buyers cannot be changed everywhere in the short run. Flexibility of individual items of expenditure is a fact that is at times considered in making the decision. But on the basis of this fact the individual user is in all cases able to arrive at an universally coordinated decision at once. Such a coordinating process requires considerable time in case of central determination of goal.

42. Extramarginal value estimates of goods also become visible in price reactions, as prosperity increases.

43. It will usually be a case of decline in prosperity, since the set tasks, as a rule, represent the maximum program, in the effort to use all reserves for production to capacity, rarely is more accomplished than is required, and because of the stimulation effect.

44. For example, Erich Welter, *Incorrect and Correct Planning* (G), Heidelberg 1954, pp. 50 f., 107.

45. This pertains especially in case of a war economy. In view of lack of insight into these relationships, which actually make impossible attaining the economic goals, by applying purely financial guidance methods during war or in particular emergencies, the criticism becomes aimless, that Eucken and Welter direct against the guidance methods of the war economy, and which, with some reservations, must be understood also for such situations as recommendation of a market economy, a purely financial guidance system. (Cf. Eucken, *Principles, op. cit.*, pp. 118 f., in connection with pp. 73-77, 84 ff., 101 f.; et al.)

46. Cf. the end of the preceding chapter (Illusion of Nominal Income).

47. Practically, they represent the area of chief applicability of planned economy; the most important case is that of the war economy.

48. It should likewise be pointed out that normal calculation, coming under the concept "Schematizing" (*Schematisierung*) which, as will be shown in the following chapter, plays an important role in the Soviet Union, is not excluded by such planning principles. Normal calculation need not be an average cost reckoning; it is also conceivable as a "schematized" marginal cost and marginal product calculation.

49. The following circumstance works in the same direction: the conception of goals can usually not take place with the aid of financial criteria, but must be material, since it is a function of anticipated future purposes that are not yet adequately expressed in the present purposive system. And even where present financial magnitudes, in general, indicate requisite goal-setting such as cost margins or unsatisfied effective financial demand, they do not yet indicate the extent of the required investment, which results from the coordination of the newly shaped system of ends and means by means of the investments. Thus it would seem that what was established above for the planning of community economic need also pertains to long-term investment planning. Material planning comes first; however, for the sake of achieving the best possible aggregate coordination, it must be converted into financial magnitudes, but since this conversion necessarily is achieved incompletely, control and correction by way of material goal-setting remains unavoidable in individual cases.

50. For example, Eucken, *Principles, op. cit.*, pp. 101 f.

51. The preceding chapter, "The Differing Altitude Toward Use of Financial Magnitudes as Lead Criteria."

52. V. D'jačenko, "Khozraschet as Socialistic Economic Method" (R), *op. cit.*, p. 14. (G. tr.), *Soviet Science*, 1951, p. 183; et al.

53. D'jačenko, *op. cit.*, p. 17.

54. Harry Schwartz, *Russia's Soviet Economy, op. cit.,* pp. 184 f.; et al.

55. A valuable start in this direction, relating particularly to the years 1934-41, appears in the work of David Granick, *Management of the Industrial Firm in the U.S.S.R.,* New York, 1954. I should like to recommend the subject matter of this study very strongly to the reader, to supplement the present work. Noteworthy is the very different formation of the relationships in separate industrial branches, as well as in large and smaller enterprises. Granick pertains primarily, but not exclusively, to the relationships in heavy and machine industry.

56. The cited data relate, in part, to different periods of time; for the large comprehensive presentations depend extensively on material from the last pre-war years. But as far as can be observed, no essential change in principle has taken place since then. Where such a change becomes apparent, it will be indicated.

57. Occasionally the supply plans are drawn up by top management, according to their own judgment, if the orders from the enterprises do not arrive in time. Frequent subsequent changes in production plans operate similarly. All these deviations and changes are actually not considered any longer in the supply plans once approved. In this connection cf. Davies, "The Reappraisal. . . . " *op. cit.,* p. 314; et al.

58. R. W. Davies, "The Builders' Conference," in *Soviet Studies,* 1954-55, Vol. 6, p. 448.

59. John Miller, "The Industrial Conference," in *Soviet Studies,* 1955-56, Vol. 7, p. 209.

60. Davies, "The Builders' Conference," *op. cit.,* p. 448.

61. M. Michajlov, "As to Reserves of Prime Cost Reduction in Industrial Production," *op. cit.,* p. 54. A. Zverev (the Minister of Finance) also complains that in drawing up plans of prime costs, enterprises and also ministries (!) deliberately increase the input norms of material and labor,

and thus "create artificial reserves" in prime cost plans (cf. A. Zverev, "The Reign of Thrift and Strengthening of Khozraschet" (R), in *Planned Economy*, 1953, No. 3, p. 19).

62. V. Lipsic, "Ways of Improving the Planning of Prime Costs of Industrial Production," *op. cit.*, p. 25.

63. *Ibid.*, p. 26. For further illustrations cf. V. Lavrov, "Ruble Control" *op. cit.*, p. 62. The delay in the delivery of the plans has particular significance in this connection, as previously mentioned.

64. "Organization of Intra-Plant Khozraschet" (R). (G tr.), *op. cit.*, pp. 65 f.

65. Lipsic, *op. cit.*, p. 26.

66. P. Podšivalenko, "Ways of Strengthening Khozraschet and Financial Control in Building Concerns" (R), in *Planned Economy*, 1952, No. 4, p. 63.

67. G. Bienstock, S. M. Schwarz, A. Yugow, *Management in Russian Industry and Agriculture*, *op. cit.*, p. 53, and especially David Granick, *Management of the Industrial Firm in the U.S.S.R.*, *op. cit.*, pp. 71 f.

68. N. N. Rovinskij, *The State Budget of the U.S.S.R.* (R), 2 vols. Moscow, 1949-50 (G tr.), *Soviet Science* Supp. 21, 35 Berlin, 1951-53, Part 2, pp. 61 f., 111.

69. B. Sokolov, "Some Questions as to the Economy of Investment Structure" (R), in *Problems of Economics*, 1950, No. 10, p. 24.

70. Preceding chapter, "Introduction of Money Calculation."

71. The division of goods and the method of regulation and terminology have changed in the course of time and apparently are also different for producers' goods and consumers' goods. Cf. for producers' goods particularly Granick, *op. cit.*, pp. 135 f., 296-302; for consumer goods, Bettelheim, *The Soviet Economy*, *op. cit.*, pp. 261 ff.; et al.

72. Lokšin, "Questions as to Planning," *op. cit.*, pp. 46 f. (Excerpts in Schwartz, *op. cit.*, pp. 161 f.)

73. B. I. Caplan, "The Organization and Control of Soviet Internal Trade" in *Soviet Studies*, Vol. 5, 1953/54, p. 66.

74. Schwartz, *op. cit.,* p. 188.
75. Preceding chapter, "Introduction of Money Calculation," as well as Bienstock et al., *op. cit.,* pp. 60 f.
76. Granick, *op. cit.,* pp. 138 f., 140 f.
77. Now ministries.
78. Bienstock, et al., *op. cit.,* pp. 62-63 f., as well as Granick, *op. cit.,* pp. 141-147; et al.
79. Cf. the opinion of H. Schwartz, *op. cit.,* p. 189.
80. Schwartz (*op. cit.,* pp. 445-454) explains in detail the history of the attempts to guide the free flow of labor forces into the channel provided by the plan and decribes its failure. (Cf. also Solomon M. Schwarz, *Labor Classes and Labor Policy in the Soviet Union* (G), Hamburg 1953, especially Chapter 3). Recently complaint was again heard that "fluctuation in labor forces is simply unbearable." Cf. V. Maljugin and V. Pisarevskij, "Urgent Questions as to Industrial Building Construction" (R), in *Communist,* Moscow, 1954, No. 8. (G) in *East Problems,* 1954, 6th yr., p. 1211. Likewise difficulties owing to free mobility of labor, together with resultant inequitable adjustment of wages and working conditions, were repeatedly reflected in occasional press observations and reports. Cf. for example the article by F. Loginov in *Pravda,* Oct. 25, 1954, (G abst.) in *East Problems,* 1954, 6th yr., pp. 1903-1904; et al.
81. According to the decree of Apr. 25, 1956, cf. the report "Government Measures at the Time of the Congress," in *Soviet Studies,* 1956-57, Vol. 8, pp. 110 f. Financial disadvantages continue to be connected with change in place of employment.
82. This will be deveolped in more detail in the following chapter.
83. A. Gordin, "Price and Price Formation in the U.S.S.R." (R), *Bol'ševik,* Moscow, 1951, No. 7, p. 63; et al.
84. According to Rovinskij, et al., op. cit., 253 ff.; et al.
85. L. Majzenberg, "The System of Wholesale Prices and

Strengthening of Khozrasčet." (R), *Planned Economy,* 1950 No. 6, p. 68 f.

86. cf. Rovinskij, *The State Budget, op. cit.,* part 1, p. 176; part 2, p. 105; et al.

87. Bienstock, et al., *op. cit.,* p. 9; et al.

88. Cf. Chapter 1, "Economic Goal-Setting," as well as B. Mirošničenko, "Planning of Industrial Production," *op. cit.,* p. 438 f.

89. Thus far according to Rovinskij, *The State Budget, op. cit.,* part 1, pp. 114 f.; et al.

90. B. Smechov "Planning Industrial Construction" (R) *Planned Economy,* 1951, No. 4, (according to *Soviet Studies*) Vol. 3, 1951-52, pp. 453 f.; et al.

91. Bienstock, et al., *op. cit.,* pp. 53 f.

92. G. Grossman, "Scarce Capital and Soviet Doctrine," in *The Quarterly Journal of Economics,* 1953, Vol. 67, pp. 314 f.

93. Rovinskij, *The State Budget, op. cit.,* part 1, pp. 157-163; et al.

94. V. M. Batyrev and V. K. Sitnin, *Organization and Planning of the Finances of Socialist Industry, op. cit.,* pp. 100-111; et al.

95. *Ibid.,* p. 107; et al.

96. Rovinskij, *The State Budget, op. cit.,* part 1, pp. 150, 154-157; et al.

97. More about this later; it should be mentioned here that efforts are made in other ways to reduce the estimated amounts in the handbooks; all participants and authorized agencies vigorously undertake crossing out and reducing of items. Projecting organizations even receive premiums, dependent on achieved reduction of estimated amounts. This often produces the reverse result, in that the authorized investment means are inadequate to coveer the actually required expenditures.

98. The practical significance of this view, especially with reference to material and machine supplies, is indicated in the frequent complaint as to such excessive supplies.

99. Rovinskij, *The State Budget, op. cit.,* part 2, p. 111; et al.

100. The relationship between profit and profit tax in connection with the analysis of the components of price will be presented in more detail subsequently.

101. According to Schwartz, *op. cit.,* p. 425; et al.

102. Concerning depreciation, cf. Bienstock, et al., *op. cit.,* p. 78.

103. Rovinskij, *The State Budget, op. cit.,* part 1, pp. 384 f.

104. Batyrev and Sitnin, *op. cit.,* p. 121; et al.

105. Rovinskij, *The State Budget, op. cit.,* part 1, pp. 174 f.; part 2, pp. 105 f.

106. Batyrev and Sitnin, *op. cit.,* pp. 119, 159, 162 f.; et al.

107. Accordingly, financing a project with allotments from the budget, inter alia, is required, where the project has to be completed under all circumstances without considering the extent to which economic organization can provide an accumulation. (Rovinskij, *The State Budget, op. cit.,* part 1, p. 157).

108. Dobb, *Soviet Economic Development Since 1917, op. cit.* (1st ed. 1949), p. 381.

109. Rovinskij, *The State Budget, op. cit.,* part 1, pp. 148 f., 185.

110. John Miller, "Comment on Smechov," *Soviet Studies* Vol. 3, p. 449; Davies, "The Reappraisal . . . ," *op. cit., p.* 319; et al.

111. Rovinskij, *The State Budget, op. cit.,* part 1, pp. 149, 196-201, as well as Russian edition of 1951, pp. 205 ff.

112. Miller, "The Industrial Conference," *op. cit.,* pp. 206 f.; et al.

113. Davies, "Economic Incentives I," *Soviet Studies,* Vol. 7, 1955-56, p. 461; et al.

114. The expenditures for construction and maintenance of workers' own homes were also defrayed from the indicated quota of the director's fund. The means in the staple commodity were thus to be used entirely to expand and improve commodity production by the divisions using them.

115. Batyrev and Sitnin, *op. cit.,* p. 129; et al.

116. Davies, The Reappraisal, *op. cit.,* p. 319.

117. P. Podšivalenko, *op. cit.*, p. 62; et al.

118. Rovinskij, *The State Budget, op. cit.*, part 1, p. 164.

119. *Ibid.*, part 2, pp. 331-334.

120. Bienstock, et al., *op. cit.*, p. 9.

121. The following chapter, "Viewpoints of Price Regulation."

122. A. I. Baumgol'c, "On the Question as to the Effectiveness of Investments" (R), in *Bulletin of the Acad. of Sci., SSSR* 1950, No. 6, pp. 449 ff.

123. The Chief Administration for Construction of Water Power Stations.

124. There is an error in original here; profitability of the project, 7%, is higher than the minimum profitability, 4 to 6.6%, called for here.

125. The "return flow period" is the reciprocal value of the coefficient of effectiveness.

126. Moreover, the effectiveness norms for planning water power stations are differentiated, according to the degree of completed opening up of the area, as well as in the presence of local sources of energy. The lowest norms, which thus make possible the greatest capital intensity, are employed in so-called pioneer territories of the far north. Baumgol'c, *op. cit.*, p. 449.

127. Planning Division of Fuel Power Plants in the Ministry of Power Plants.

128. *Ibid.*, p. 451.

129. P. Denisov, "Practical Testing is the Best Control of a Method" (R), *Problems of Economies,* 1951, No. 1, pp. 112-119, especially 115, excerpt reproduced in *Soviet Studies,* 1952-53, No. 4, pp. 346-348.

130. As to the existing disproportionalities in equipping individual factories, cf. P. Ivanov, "Planning the Utilization of Productive Possibilities" (R), *Planned Economy,* 1949, No. 4, pp. 16 ff.

131. Batyrev and Sitnin, *op. cit.*, p. 129.

Chapter 4

1. Occasionally the development resulted from the influence of newly introduced products into the price system; thus prices were apparently not fixed to correspond with the 1926 prices of similar products but on the basis of prevailing cost conditions. Here the inflationary effect of increasing wages in the course of inflation, on the one hand, and the apparent choice of a period burdened with high initial costs as decisive for price setting, on the other hand, became operative, as well as the practice of concerns to shift costs as far as possible from newly introduced comparable products, and hence included in lowered costs plans, to noncomparable items. Cf. Jasny, *The Soviet Price System,* pp. 93-143, especially pp. 96 f., 103 ff.; et al.

2. Until 1949 they were expressed in the prices of 1926-27.

3. V. D'jačenko, "Khozraschet as Socialistic Economic Method," *op. cit.;* (G) *Soviet Science,* 1951, p. 184; et al.

4. G. Drampjan, N. Fedotov, "Planning of Gross Output of Industry in Comparable Prices" (R) in *Planned Economy,* 1952, No. 1, pp. 76 f.; Alec Nove; "The New Planning Prices (R), Comment on the stated work of Drampjan et al. in *Soviet Studies,* 1953-54, Vol. 5, pp. 84-89; Jasny, *op. cit.,* pp. 129-132; current prices, in general were apparently intended to take their place. Because of difficulties growing out of frequent price changes (cf. Nove, *op. cit.,* p. 86) there was soon a return to basing an essential part of planning procedure, namely, planning "gross production," for some time on prices prevailing at the time ("gross production" includes an increase in quantity of unfinished products and the like; it is the decisive magnitude in reports of plan fulfillment). First the prices of January 1952 were chosen; since 1956 they are those of July 1, 1955. Commodity production (not considering changes in the amount of inventory of unfinished products), on the other hand, is planned in current prices. cf. Nove, *op. cit.;* et al.

5. The use of the term "profit" (*pribyl'*) must not mislead to the assumption, as happens at times with Western authors and even with Russians themselves, that the term thus designated serves the function of profit according to Western theory. Planned profit is primarily a tax element: it depends on the difference between costs and prices, established according to plan by the State. By far the major part of profits enters the State budget to meet public needs. . . . According to the new official manual, *Political Economy* (Moscow, 1954, pp. 473 f. and 476) the total tax share in price (profit and turnover tax) is to be designated as pure profit or social net income, and the share remaining with the enterprise as pure profit (net income) of State enterprise, while the share going to the State (withdrawal of profit and turnover tax) as centralized pure profit of the State. The terms "profit" and "turnover tax" are called incorrect.

6. Thus far, according to Gordin, "Price and Price Formation in the U.S.S.R.," *op. cit.*, pp. 65 f.; et al.

7. The procedure in calculating monetary prime costs, based on material data, is presented in P. E. Zolotuchin, *Production Accounting and Calculation in Local Industry* (R), Moscow, 1951, pp. 11-19, 33-36. Cf. also Majzenberg, "Price Formation in the Economy of the U.S.S.R." (R) Moscow, 1953, pp. 101-117; et al.

8. Baykov, *Development of the Soviet Economic System*, *op. cit.*, pp. 295 f., et al.

9. A. Gordin, "Price and Price Formation in the U.S.S.R.," *op. cit.*, pp. 68 f. cf. also Majzenberg, "Price Formation," *op. cit.*, pp. 128-132. Majzenberg also mentions the interesting manner in which "differential profits" arising out of particularly favorable "natural and transporation conditions," such as in providing lumber, are withdrawn; this takes place by means of the so-called lumber purchase money, which is to be paid "as a sort of rent" in addition to taxes. In certain special cases, otherwise, direct higher prices are permitted to certain enterprises. With reference to differ-

entiated transfer prices, Baykov (*op. cit.*, pp. 292-296) states that this method had been employed from 1928 to 1936, and then was displaced by the assessment procedure. However, the method of transfer prices, according to statements by Gordin and Majzenberg, still pertains. Eventually it is related to the method of distributing goods in the particular industrial branch (cf. "Position of the Enterprise in the Soviet Guidance System" of the preceding chapter). A price differentiation, in the indicated sense, is possible only for goods of "fund production" and "quota products." I could not determine whether the "transfer prices" were identical with the "wholesale prices of the enterprise" or whether the former, relative to the latter, already represented a uniform price.

10. The concept ground rent is here used in the broader sense, which includes the price of all treasures of the soil that can be appropriated, natural resources and natural forces whose value has not yet been increased by input of labor and capital. Cf. for example V. Stackelberg, *Principles, op. cit.*, pp. 7, 261.

11. Jasny, *Price System, op. cit.*, p. 69, in this connection speaks of a special assessment per ton of crude oil extracted or per felled tree. The lumber purchase money just mentioned (footnote 9), ultimately identical with the latter, actually represents a kind of location and quality rent. In the low prices of compulsory agricultural deliveries, on the other hand, as Jasny states in disagreeing with Dobb (*Soviet Economic Development, op. cit.*, p. 284) there is no concealed ground rent payment but a tax element. (Jasny, *op. cit.*, pp. 50, 69 f.)

12. Rovinskij, *The State Budget, op. cit.*, pp. 117-142, 151-157, as well as an extensive literature pertaining to "accelerating the turnover of circulating media." The fact that interest on short-term credit is added naturally stimulates the indicated cost comparison. However, this effect is overshadowed, by far, by the institutional controls of and the concom-

mitant conditions for granting credit. A first condition for granting credit is that it is a matter of planned or otherwise legally established credit need. If these prerequisites exist, there is not too much worry about the status of costs. And where credit is granted in violation of these prerequisites, it usually pertains to a need that has arisen because of non-fulfillment of production plans or cost plans, i.e., a temporary need, where no interest is required.

13. Baumgol'c, "On the Question as to the Effectiveness of Investments," *op. cit.,* p. 449.

14. The question as to the development of agricultural income will be omitted here, since the emphasis in this study is on industrial price formation and particularly on prices of producers' goods. Price and distribution policy in the Soviet Union relative to agriculture is well presented by Gerhard Lenschow, "Methods and Effects of Price Policy in the Soviet Union, 1913-1937," (G), in *World Economic Archive,* 1945, Vol. 61, pp. 116-127; cf. also Jasny, *op. cit.,* pp. 46-63.

15. Insofar as it pertains as a rule to piece rates, in connection with labor norms, which set normal performance for every type of labor.

16. H. Schwartz, *Russia's Soviet Economy. op. cit.,* pp. 457 ff.; et al.

17. H. Schwartz, *op. cit.,* pp. 456 f., referring to Stalin's speech of June 13, 1931 ("Questions of Leninism" (G), from 11th Russian edition, Moscow, 1946, pp. 405 ff.). Later there was an opposite tendency. The trend toward a general rise in wages owing to inflation appeared primarily in the form of upgrading of lower qualification grades, in view of institutional obstacles forbidding wage increases. Details in this chapter, "Significance of Inflation."

18. Bettelheim, *The Soviet Economy, op. cit.,* p. 166; et al.

19. H. Schwartz, *op. cit.,* p. 464. Bettelheim, *op. cit.,* pp. 180 ff. The question as to the rationality of the wage structure in the Soviet Union was basis of a recent discussion between P. Wiles ("Are Adjusted Rubles Rational?" in *Soviet Studies*

1955-56, 7, pp. 145 ff.) and D. R. Hodgman ("Measuring Soviet Industrial Expansion"; a reply, in *Soviet Studies,* 1956-57, 8, pp. 36 ff.) Cf. also Joan Robinson ("Mr. Wiles' Rationality," *op. cit.,* p. 271). I agree with Hodgman that, simply from the permissive mobility of labor forces, combined with efforts to influence this mobility with the aid of wage increases, a certain trend toward rational development of wage relations must result. In refuting Joan Robinson it should be observed that such wage differences, corresponding with a condition of monetary scarcity, are not an error, but a necessary factor in a rational price system. In the first place it is not appropriate to neglect completely the significance of varying aptitude and inclination for specific activities in wage setting because of the prevailing many-sided adaptability and usefulness of industrial labor forces. Furthermore, the limited occupational mobility of trained labor forces belongs to the basically determinative factors of the prevailing labor supply, and if this results in fluctuations in evaluating the labor power of specific qualification, they are economically justified. From a purely economic point of view it is rational that occupational groups of which there is a surplus because of economic development should receive less income, while others who are drawn into scarce occupations should obtain a rent in consequence.

20. Detail later.
21. A. K. Sučkov, *Economic Nature and Basic Principles of the Organization of the Turnover Tax* (R), Moscow, 1951, pp. 20, 24; Batyrev and Sitnin, *Organization and Planning of the Finances of Socialist Industry, op. cit.,* p. 30; Baykov, *Development of the Soviet Economic System, op. cit.,* p. 375.
22. *Ibid.,* p. 376.
23. See below, "Significance of Inflation."
24. Sučkov, *op. cit.,* p. 20.
25. According to Baykov (*op. cit.,* pp. 369, 375), the turnover tax on the most important consumers' goods is withdrawn daily, otherwise preponderatingly every ten days, while

profit withdrawals are computed quarterly and are paid in monthly rates.

26. The translated German title reads "The Economic Nature and Basic Organization Principles of the Turnover Tax."

27. Sučkov, *op. cit.,* p. 35.

28. Tabulations of rates made known are found in Jasny, *op. cit.,* Appendix, Table I, pp. 164-167 (related text pp. 70-84); Schwartz, *op. cit.,* p. 417; Bienstock et al., *Management in Russian Industry and Agriculture, op. cit.,* p. 84.

29. Jasny, *op. cit.,* p. 77; Davies, "Short-term Credit in the U.S.S.R.," *op. cit.,* p. 25 with footnote 11; Schwartz, *op. cit.,* pp. 415 f.

30. This includes compulsory delivery from agriculture and the like.

31. It is not indicated in what prices they are measured; presumably they are the "1926-1927 prices." The relationships have at least not yet been distorted by including the increase from the turnover tax.

32. According to Russian statistics reproduced by Schwartz, *op. cit.,* p. 416, and Poom, "Economy, Effectiveness and Profitability in Soviet Industry," *op. cit.,* p. 160. These are derived from statistics reproduced by Jasny, *op. cit.,* pp. 110 f. (Costs of production and value of planned production for 1941 for all large industrial ministries and people's commissars are in current and "constant" prices.)

33. Rovinskij, *op. cit.,* p. 168. The relationship of wage sums to commodity production, in contrast with gross output, means that the computed 5 per cent limit of contributions to the directors' fund is not based on the labor input in the course of the year, but on delivered products; thus the part of wage payment is not considered, which increases the stock of semifinished production, and add to circulating capital (tools produced within the plant, etc.), and to intrafirm investments. (cf. E. S. Kamencier, *Organization and Planning of Socialist Industrial Plants* (R), (G tr.). Berlin, 1954, pp. 53 ff.,); et al. Moreover, "in determining unplanned profits,

a savings due to lowering costs—certain changes must be considered (increases or decreases), the appearance of which are not influenced by the enterprise. These include price changes of raw materials, semifinished products, fuel and other materials, changes in railway and other freight rates, planned substitution of important types of crude and combustible materials, changes in wage rates, wage assessments, labor norms, tax rates and bank interest, levies for communal purposes and depreciation rates, changes in delivery prices of own products, obligations that can no longer be fulfilled because of expiration of time, and resultant increase in stipulated profits" (Rovinskij, *op. cit.,* p. 169). In their present form the regulations originated in 1946 and 1948 (*ibid.,* p. 168 footnote); et al.

34. Rovinskij, *op. cit.,* part 1, p. 170.
35. Poom, *op. cit.,* p. 201, who apparently views the graduation of profit shares, in general, as determined by the "profitability" of industrial branches. In 1940 Batyrev and Sitnin (*op. cit.,* p. 44) complained about the prevailing disorder: "The still prevailing disorder in determining the height of planned profit is apparent in the size of the directors' fund in individual industrial branches. Economic branches with high planned profitability might at times obtain larger sums as deductions in favor of the directors' fund with partial fulfilling of the plan than economic branches, with lower planned profitability, which fulfill their accumulation plan. The height of the withdrawals in favor of the directors' fund in individual economic branches does not correspond sufficiently with the economic importance of these branches and their productive accomplishments. Suffice it to say that in 1938, 31 per cent of the aggregate sum of the withdrawals in favor of the directors' fund came from the foodstuffs, fish, meat, and dairy industries, 10.5 per cent from light and textile industry, and only 18.6 per cent from machine construction, mining industry, defense industry, and fuel production." However, this relationship in this respect now appears

to be more rational, first because of the graduation of the rates of participation described above, and secondly, perhaps because of removal of causes for anonymously high profits of the consumers' goods industries, namely those with runaway inflationary prices, and finally also owing to the limitations set by aggregate wage quotas.

36. Rovinskij, *op. cit.*, part 1, p. 170 f.

37. "Means of other organizations and persons, which as a result of the prevailing accounting procedure are constantly fluctuating," namely obligations to suppliers, prepaid orders of buyers, deferred wages, salaries, and the like for the current wage period; in addition, there are certain anticipated liabilities; cf. Rovinskij, *op. cit.*, part 1, pp. 135 f.

38. Cf. The preceding chapter, "Compatibility of the Material and the Financial Guiding Method."

39. Rovinskij, *op. cit.*, part 1, pp. 174 f.; part 2, pp. 105 f., as well as Schwartz, *op. cit.*, p. 417. Schwartz also surveys profits and profit withdrawals of individual industrial branches in 1940. The minimum withdrawal of 10% is also maintained with simultaneous allotments of budgetary means, in this case there are countertransfers. For details, cf. Baykov, *op. cit.*, pp. 297, 374 f.; et al.

40. As in footnote 38.

41. Batyrev and Sitnin, *op. cit.*, pp. 43 f.

42. P. Malachinov, "About Profit and Turnover Tax in the U.S.S.R." (R), *Problems of Economics,* 1954, No. 9 (G abst.) in *East Problems,* 1954, 6th yr., pp. 1834, 1835; et al.

43. A. Gordin, *op. cit.*, pp. 63 f.; et al.

44. A Zaubermann, "Economic Thought in the Soviet Union, 1. Economic Law and the Theory of Value," in *Review of Economic Studies,* Vol. XVI (1) No. 39, 1948-49, p. 2 f. The traditional assertion as to the worthwhileness (*Wertgemässigkeit*) of the price system, based on an assumed equivalence of aggregate prices and aggregate value of products in spite of divergence of individual prices, is apparent fallacy (*Sophismus*), although not always obvious to

us. It can be refuted simply by the thought that no price system is possible that does not satisfy this condition of identity of aggregate prices and aggregate values. For the statement "In this price system the prices are determined by commodity values" expresses something only if thereby it is distinguished from other price systems where that is not the case. This agreement could then be destroyed if, having been accepted for a particular price system, a single price were to be arbitrarily changed. Actually, the agreement between the two aggregate sums is not destroyed by such an arbitrary change, but only their relationship. Between value systems based on different standards there can be connections only relative to proportions, not to aggregate dimensions. Where this correspondence in proportions does not pertain, one is no longer justified in speaking of connections.

45. K. Ostravitjanov, "Socialist Planning and the Law of Value," *op. cit.*, pp. 17 ff.

46. A poor book as to intraindustrial accumulation by S. Ja. Tureckij, reviewed by A. Arakelian and P. Mstislavskij in *Problems of Economics*, 1949, No. 5, pp. 93-98.

47. Arakelian and Mstislavskij, *op. cit.*, pp. 96 f.

48. *Ibid.*, p. 97.

49. *Ibid.*, p. 97. More consistent attempts to develop a theoretically closed economic system were undertaken, particularly in connection with the effectiveness criterion, primarily by V. V. Novozilov, M. M. Protod'jakonov, and A. L. Lur'e. They were opposed with the same arguments.

50. Baykov, *op. cit.*, p. 258; et al.

51. Jasny in *American Economic Review*, 1950, Vol. 40, S. 845-863 (The article bears the title of the frequently cited monograph, "The Soviet Price System," Stanford, 1951. However, *Price System, op. cit.* subsequently will always refer to the monograph.

52. Even as the distribution of the turnover taxes in this respect, see above.

53. These were even introduced before World War II for a series of building materials (primarily cement, glass, and tile), in 1950 for heavy metals and lumber. Their further extension was being considered. Cf. F. Dobrynin, L. Kvitnickij, "For Improving Building Plans and Cost Estimates in the Building Industry" (R), in *Planned Economy*, 1950, No. 6, p. 56; Majzenberg, "The System of Wholesale Prices and the Strengthening of Chozrasčet" (R) in *Planned Economy*, 1950, No. 6, pp. 66 f.

54. Majzenberg, "The System of Wholesale Prices," p. 67; cf. p. 61, et al.

55. Dobrynin and Kvitnickij, *op. cit.*, p. 55.

56. The trade handbooks for industrial building construction drawn up on the basis of the price reform of April 1, 1936, which did not appear until after December 1, 1936, remained in use until the great price reform of 1949. The calculations were adjusted to pronounced changes in price relations by permitting all types of necessary compensations and additions. Since 1945 the price estimates of 1945, appeared beside the prices of 1936 in projecting activity, but these were only partially carried through. After the price reform of 1949 the attempt was made to base projections on current wholesale prices, but in 1950 there was return to the "price estimates of 1945." Subsequently estimates were made on the basis of 1950 prices. Thus far, according to Naum Jasny, *Soviet Prices of Producers' Goods*, Stanford, 1952, pp. 95-109; et al.

57. P. Podšivalenko, "Ways of Strengthening Khozraschet and Financial Control in Building Concerns," *op. cit.*, p. 64; et al.

58. V. Burgman, "The New Norms and Instructions for the Building Industry and Their Economic Significance" (R) in *Planned Economy*, 1955, No. 1, pp. 57 ff.

59. M. Bogolepov in *Planned Economy*, 1936, No. 5, cited by Baykov, *op. cit.*, p. 294.

60. In 1933-35 subsidies for coal amounted to 100 per cent of

price; for steel, up to 50 per cent. Jasny estimates the subsidies for 1945 at more than 40 billion rubles. Cf. Jasny,
Price System, op. cit., pp. 86 ff., and also Jasny, *Prices of Producers' Goods, op. cit.,* pp. 41 f., 47-50, 59 f., 67, 76. Furthermore, as evidence of subsidies and other financial aid policies
cf. Baykov, *op. cit.,* pp. 294 ff.; et al.

61. Rovinskij, *op. cit.,* part 1, pp. 86 f., with reference to the
order of the Council of Ministers of the U.S.S.R., July 28,
1948.

62. Jasny, in *Price System, op. cit.,* pp. 90 f., the 1951 edition
of the book by Rovinskij states that subsidies had been discontinued in 1950 (pp. 396 ff.). Nove, "Soviet National Income Statistics," pp. 260 ff., believes that the policy of low
prices of producers' goods was readopted deliberately in 1950
in connection with the overthrow of Voznesenskij again
necessitating subsidies to a certain, but minor, extent.

63. P. Vladimirov, in *Planned Economy,* 1948, No. 8, cited by
Harry Schwartz, *op. cit.,* p. 194, and Jasny, Price System, *op.
cit.,* p. 90, et al. This more recent work by Majzenberg
("Price Formation," *op. cit.*) at all events now indicates a
more correct understanding of the problem when he says
that subsidies had led to an "unnatural decrease in input
expenditures in economic branches, which are users of the
products sold at a loss," and at the same time "to an artificial reduction in the proportion of material costs in prime
costs of industrial products, which impaired the inducement
to thrift in the use of raw materials, in operating and in
supplementary items." (p. 240; cf. also p. 242).

64. Rovinskij, *op. cit.,* part 1, p. 380 f., with further references
to the procedure followed.

65. The necessity for fundamental clarification of these questions
is not diminished by the fact that practical delimiting of
such shares of costs is only very roughly possible. Realization
of economic principles always occurs with rough approximation, which is at least preferable to complete lack of principles.

66. Bogolepov, according to Baykov, *op. cit.*, p. 294; et al.

67. Cf. for example B. N. Voznesenskij, *The Wartime Economy of the U.S.S.R. in the Period of World War II* (R), Gov. Pol. Pub. House 1947, pp. 128 f.

68. For example Gordin, *op. cit.*, p. 69. "Thus in the footwear industry, the price of rubber-soled shoes is set relatively lower, in order to introduce leather substitutes in production" (naturally, what is meant is in consumption). Or Batyrev and Sitnin, *op. cit.*, p. 41; "In some cases relatively higher prices decrease demand for products which appear as luxury items; and conversely, lower prices aid in introducing many cultural products into everyday use." Majzenberg ("Price Formation," p. 155-161) recently attempted to interpret the problem more clearly.

69. Bettelheim asserts that price fixing of consumers' goods proceeds entirely from the view of regulating demand, both aggregate demand and regional demand (*op. cit.*, pp. 263 f., 433, 431 f.) However, the primary emphasis here appears to be placed on regulating aggregate, demand including total regional demand.

70. Here follows a long series of factual illustrations pertaining to the use of price differentials, fixed by the central authority, to achieve economies in the use of scarce materials and to encourage the use of cheaper substitutes (p. 152, paragraph 2, line 6 to bottom of p. 153 have been omitted from translation).

71. Maurice Dobb, "Practice and Theory of Railway Rates," in *Soviet Studies,* 1949-50, Vol. 1, p. 313-315; et al.

72. Majzenberg, "The System of Wholesale Prices," *op. cit.*, pp. 61 f.

73. Dobb, *op. cit.*, excepting rates for coal transport from Kuznets to Magnitogorsk.

74. Thus far according to Majzenberg, "The System of Wholesale Prices," *op. cit.*, p. 62; et al. Promoting water transportation is apparently more recent, and moreover, only necessary in this form, because of the "incapability of organizing

cheaper water transportation" about which Jasny states (*Prices of Producers' Goods, op. cit.,* p. 51), "The 1941 tariffs implied . . . only a small saving in the transport of Baku oil to Moscow by water and rail rather than by all-rail, and apparently a loss for Grozny under the same conditions."

75. Majzenberg, "The System of Wholesale Prices," *op. cit.,* pp. 66 f.; et al. Uniform prices for the entire area, without consideration of production or consumption of buyer, pertain particularly for consumers' goods, where transportation costs relative to price are of minor importance, as for example textiles, shoes, tobacco products, as well as for some important producers' goods, for example rolled steel (iron plates) since 1951. Otherwise there is a differentiation, on the one hand, according to locations of production, where individual production areas show very different costs of production, and transportation costs represent a large part of the price, as particularly in the case of coal. (The same holds for electric energy.) On the other hand, there is a differentiation according to marketing areas, by forming so-called price zones. Zone prices, in the first instance, are graduated according to differences in transportation costs, where, however, the differences may be increased or diminished, with a view to realizing other guiding effects. Very considerable differences in transportation costs within a zone are not expressed in the price, "but only in the accumulations of the marketing organizations of industry and trade, and also in the turnover tax." Such differentiation is found primarily with foodstuffs and crude oil products, but also with other industrial products; for example, there are three zones for grain products, two for crude oil products. Crude oil products illustrate diminishing price differences.

76. Majzenberg, "The System of Wholesale Prices," *op. cit.,* p. 67. Cf. furthermore, if finally the costs of commodity transport are not considered in industrial wholesale prices, it reduces the possibility of using transportation costs in the interest

of rational organization of transport considerably. Insofar as transportation costs concern the buyers of production, directly, there is no incentive for the sender to lower transportation costs" (pp. 66 f.); et al.

77. See above (Dobb, "Practice and Theory," *op. cit.*, pp. 313-315.)

78. Batyrev and Sitnin, *op. cit.*, p. 40.

79. *Ibid.*, p. 42 already quoted previously).

80. Further illustration omitted p. 157, paragraph 2, line 12 f.

81. S. K. Tatur, "Chozrasčet and Profitability," (R), Acad. of Sci. U.S.S.R. *Izvestia, Dept. of Econ. Phil. and Law,* No. 3 (1950), p. 170, cited by Harry Schwartz, *op. cit.*, p. 195.

82. Majzenberg, "The System of Wholesale Prices," *op. cit.*, p. 61.

83. Gorin, *op. cit.*, p. 69. Cf. also p. 64, "Thus, even if production of a ton of crude oil requires less social expenditures than the production of a ton of anthracite, the price of crude oil products would have to be higher than the price of coal, in order to stimulate economic ultilization of crude oil products." Likewise Majzenberg, "Price Formation," pp. 119 f., 159 f., 174 f.

84. The so-called execution of building projects by contracting out to plant construction enterprises, in contrast with construction by the management that will subsequently operate the plant.

85. Krylov, "Against the Bourgeois Methodology in Questions of Economy of Transport" (R) (Book review), in *Planned Economy* 1949, No. 4, p. 89: It is known that in spite of the cheapness of water transport, a considerable part of goods is shipped by rail, even on parallel-running main transportation lines. . . . The author should have shown, in particular, that the insufficient development of water transport depends on systematic excess in assembling time of goods for water transport, irregular work at the loading points, prevailing disruption of harbor activity in numerous in-

stances, leading enterprises located near main water transport arteries to make too little use of water transport.

86. Cf. also the following section.

87. Gerhard Mackenroth ("Socialist Economic Order" (G) in *World Economic Archive,* 1949, Vol. 63, especially pp. 187 f., 212) opposes this; however, his arguments in this respect can be refuted.

88. The card game similé "Schwarzen Peter" used by the author is untranslatable since this game does not exist in English. The game of "Hearts" approximates it.

89. Cf. the quotes above, p. 17 of mimeograph. Also the intended guidance effect of "net wholesale delivered prices" aims at guidance effects of the distribution of a given total amount, and not of the total amount of production and transportation achievement.

90. Alec Cairncross, "The Moscow Conference," in *Soviet Studies,* 1952-53, Vol. 4, p. 121.

91. Jasny, *Prices of Producers' Goods, op. cit.,* p. 52.

92. Thus far, according to Jasny, *Prices of Producers' Goods, op. cit.,* pp. 81 f.

93. A further illustration pertaining to the irrational price relations in the development of lime and cement production, based on Jasny's study, has been omitted from the translation: p. 165, paragraph 2.

94. Majzenberg, "The System of Wholesale Prices," *op. cit.,* p. 65.

95. Jasny, *Prices of Producers' Goods, op. cit.,* p. 82.

96. *Ibid.,* pp. 77 f.

97. Further illustration omitted, p. 166, paragraph 3 to p. 167, paragraph 1, line 3.

98. Baykov, *op. cit.,* p. 259; cf. also p. 262.

99. Harry Schwartz, *op. cit.,* p. 192.

100. Further illustrations of wide variations in margins of profits on similar items, cited by the author, have been omitted: p. 168, paragraph 1, lines 8 to 30.

101. Thus far, according to Majzenberg, "The System of Wholesale prices," *op. cit.*, p. 68

102. It should be noted that other organizational defects also exist in interfirm cooperation that lead to actual cost increases. The primary reason is the provincial egoism (*Ressortegoismus*) of management of individual ministries. "Until the ministries were combined, machine building enterprises received individual parts and trimmings from factories in remote regions, within the area of productive cooperation (within their own ministries), while an enterprise of another ministry, but located nearer, had excess capacity and could produce the products satisfactorily." ("The Reorganization of the Ministries—Measure of Great Governmental and Economic Importance" (R) [lead article] in *Planned Economy*, 1953, No. 2, pp. 5 f.) Majzenberg gives an illustration where cast steel plates move in interfirm cooperation from Voronež by way of Odessa to Slavjansk; i.e., 1400 air km., criss-cross through a major industrial territory. Added to these superfluous transport expenditures is the fact that the factories of other ministries were equipped with assembly line construction of such parts, and thus have considerably lower costs. Majzenberg cites a further case, where a factory of the aircraft production ministry figured for delivered parts 20 times as much as similar products cost at the mining industry ministry. (Majzenberg, "The System of Wholesale Prices," pp. 64 f.)

103. Baykov, *op. cit.*, p. 370; Maurice Dobb, "A Note on Turnover Tax and Prices" in *Soviet Studies*, 1952-53, Vol. 4, pp. 273 f.; et al.

104. Cairncross, *op. cit.*, p. 121; Joan Robinson, "Theory and Practice of Planning" (Review) *Soviet Studies*, 1952-53, Vol. 4, p. 57. Particularly important is her reference to the rigidity of turnover tax rates.

105. To illustrate the introduction of the turnover tax as regulating instrument the fact may be noted that turnover taxes on producers' goods relate primarily to such products,

when price increases are intended to curtail consumption. This also pertains to an illustration given by Jasny, *Price System, op. cit.*, p. 85, of maintaining a stable price (of rye bread, 1940) in spite of increased costs, by lowering the turnover tax. On the other hand, there is the relative rigidity of tax rates which, however, according to Jasny's observation, is not as great as that of prices.

106. The following two reproduced series are, strictly speaking, obviously not comparable. They have both been compiled on the basis of questionable supporting data, and the price series in general pertains to only a small, although important segment of the over-all price development. I should not like to venture an opinion as to how far it is therefore possible to draw conclusions as to the development of real wages from a combination of the two series, as Harry Schwartz (*op. cit.*, pp. 461 f.) has attempted to do, although with reservations. Other estimates are far different in both directions; cf. for example M. C. Kaser, "Soviet Statistics of Wages and Prices," in *Soviet Studies*, 1955-56, Vol. 7, pp. 246 ff. (for further estimates). For our purposes it is here merely a matter of observing the parallel development of prices and wages.

107. Jasny, *Price System, op. cit.*, p. 23, compiled or computed from various sources. Almost the same sequence in figures compiled by Harry Schwartz, *op. cit.*, p. 460. Sources of the latest statistics in Jasny, *op. cit.*, pp. 27-40.

108. Schwartz, *op. cit.*, p. 378. Details as to methods of computation, and reservations. Price increase of foodstuffs is presumably greater than that of the aggregate of consumers' goods; on the other hand, the prices in free and black markets were considerably higher. Price increases of producers' goods varied considerably and were irregular with reference to individual items. A compilation of individual illustrations is made by Jasny, *Price System, op. cit.*, p. 168 (Table 2 in appendix) as well as of prices of producers' goods, cf. *Prices of Producers' Goods, op. cit.*, (The most

important illustrations are reproduced in what follows.) (They have, however, been contracted considerably in the translation, since they do not appear to add to an understanding of the general thesis of the author and, at best, merely quote from secondary sources.)

109. Kazer, *op. cit.;* Jasny, "The Soviet Budget, 1956," in *East-Europe Economy,* 1956, 1st yr., pp. 33-40.

110. Jasny, *Price System, op. cit.,* p. 14; cf. Dobb, *Development, op. cit.* (1st ed.) pp. 240, 278; et al.

111. *Pravda,* Feb. 4, 1955, abstract translated in *East Problems,* 1955, 7th yr., pp. 329 f.; cf. furthermore, I. Suprunenko, "Reserves of Lower Building Costs," (R), in *Planned Economy,* 1953, No. 5, pp. 51 f. (with tables).

112. Illustration omitted, p. 173, paragraph 1, lines 17-21.

113. Maljugin and Pisarevskij "Urgent Problems," quoted from *East Problems, op. cit.,* p. 1211.

114. Dobb, *Soviet Economic Development, op. cit.,* pp. 240, 278; S. N. Prokopovicz, *Russia's Economy under the Soviets* (G), Zurich, New York, 1944, pp. 307 f.

115. The one expresses itself in the progressive tendency toward increased wage differences. Cf. Solomon M. Schwarz, *Labor Classes, op. cit.,* pp. 215 ff., the other contradicts directly the known pressure to increase norms, and again shows, that, in this respect, enterprises had more freedom than accords with the basic idea of the system.

116. According to Davies, "The Reappraisal," *op. cit.,* p. 325; cf. also Miller, The Industrial Conference, *op. cit.,* p. 207.

117. Jasny reports concerning this in *Prices of Producers' Goods, op. cit.,* pp. 74, 77 f.

118. According to illustrations in Jasny, *ibid.,* pp. 75, 77. Cf. also what was said above concerning the development of black market conditions.

119. Jasny, *Price System, op. cit.,* pp. 22-26.

120. *Ibid.,* p. 35.

121. Here follows a long list of illustrations based on Jasny's studies, showing that price changes of producers' goods

were made only at long intervals, but then in large jumps, frequently twofold and threefold increases, while consumers' goods prices were changed oftener, but there were also years of stable prices of consumers' goods between periods of frequent changes; p. 177, paragraph 2, line 2 to p. 181, inclusive, have been omitted from this translation.

122. Jasny, *ibid.*, p. 132, footnote 41; et al.

123. In a consistently constructed financial value system, the distribution of the burden of taxes must be neutral as to value, i.e., it may change prices only proportionally. But in the area of consumers' goods turnover tax rates fluctuate widely; cf. illustrations given by Jasny, *ibid.*, Appendix Table 1, pp. 164-167; et al.

124. For example, supplementary taxation of agriculture (in price of fertilizer).

125. These irrational profit and loss spreads were a basic reason for the price reform and currency stabilization, even though establishing a correctly coordinated price system was obviously not intended to be the actual goal.

Index

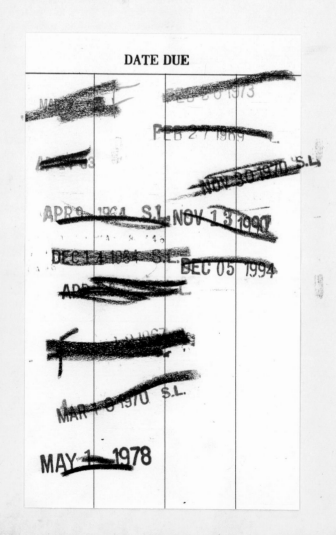